THE RECIPE

A US Marine's Mindset
For Success

JAKE COSME

© 2021 Jake Cosme

Published by Dawn Publishing
www.dawnbates.com
The moral right of the author has been asserted.
For quantity sales or media enquiries, please contact the publisher at the website address above.

Cataloguing-in-Publication entry is available from the British Library.
ISBN:
978-1-913973-24-7 (paperback)
978-1-913973-25-4 (ebook)

Book cover design – Miladinka Milic

All rights reserved. No part of this book may be reproduced, stored in a retrieval system, communicated or transmitted in any form or by means without written permission. All inquiries should be made to the publisher at the above address.

Disclaimer: The material in this publication is of the nature of general comment only and does not represent professional advice. It is not intended to provide specific guidance for particular circumstances and should not be relied on as the basis for any decision to take action or not to take action on any matters which it covers.

ALSO PUBLISHED BY DAWN PUBLISHING:

Standing in Strength – Inspirational Stories of Power Unleashed by Laarni Mulvey (2021)

Becoming the Champion – V1 Awareness by Korey Carpenter (2020)

Unlocked by Carmelle Crinnion (2020)

Break Down to Wake Up by Jocelyn Bellows (2020)

Becoming Annie by Dawn Bates (2020)

The Democ'Chu Series by Nath Brye:

Slave Boy – Book One (2020)

Blood Child – Book Two (2021)

The Trilogy of Life Itself by Dawn Bates:

Friday Bridge – Becoming a Muslim, Becoming Everyone's Business (2nd Edition, 2017)

Walaahi – A First-hand Account of Living Through the Egyptian Uprising and Why I Walked Away From Islaam (2017)

Crossing The Line – A Journey of Purpose and Self-Belief (2017)

The Sacral Series by Dawn Bates:

Moana – One Woman's Journey Back to Self (2020)

Leila – A life Renewed One Blank Canvas at a Time (2020)

Pandora – Melting the Ice One Dive at a Time (2021)

DEDICATED TO THE MEMORY OF

Major Elizabeth Betsy Kealey, USMC
Major Taj Sareen, USMC
First Lieutenant Jason D. Mann, USMC
First Lieutenant Joshua L. Booth, USMC
TSGT Osvaldo R. Cosme Jr, USAF

CONTENTS

Foreword	ix
Gratitude	xiii
Preface	xv
Introduction to "The Struggle"	xix
Prologue	1
1. How It Started	7
2. Prep School	15
3. The Academy	21
4. Usmc	31
5. The Downfall	49
6. The Wakeup Call	63
The Recipe	75
Ingredient I – Your Purpose	77
Ingredient II – Your Want	87
Ingredient III – Your Intention	101
Ingredient IV – Your Habits	109
Ingredient V – Your Affirmations	117
Ingredient VI – Your Strengths	125
Closing	133
Epilogue – How It's Going	145
The Downfall of Veterans	151
My Recipe	153
My Self Evaluation	159
What Is Hustle?	163
About the Author	165
Dawn Publishing	167

FOREWORD

Reading this book has impacted me in a number of ways, not just as someone who is dedicated to being of service to humanity, but as a woman, a mother, and a friend. When my friend Pete Canalichio told me he wanted to introduce me to an ex-Marine who wanted to write a book, I will be honest, I was hesitant, and yet intrigued. As a woman who was married to an Arab, the mother of two Palestinian children, and someone who is anti-military for a variety of reasons, my political and humanitarian triggers went into overdrive.

Knowing Pete had read my books, I trusted he would refer someone who not only would I get along well with, but someone who's story would be one I would be interested in working on and publishing, because not just any book gets my fire on its spine!

Over the years, those of us watching American politics will have seen American go to war with almost every part of the world since its inception. Wars within its own land mass, wars within its own states and within its own forces. We've watched as friendly fire has become expected and seen how those who have served their country have been dismissed without a second thought.

The increasing number of veterans spiraling into drugs, drink, despair and ending up on the streets of almost every city in America, their families torn apart and the horrifying memories visiting them with every blink of their eyes. There are numerous initiatives around the world where veterans support veterans, but due to a lack of funding and support, these initiatives fall by the wayside and disillusionment replaces hope and justice for the millions of veterans discarded by the US government without a second thought.

Jake has shown me that the imperialistic, white-dominated military and industrialized political complex, which needs to keep going to war to stay in business, is not the reality for those who choose to serve their country. It is in fact the opposite, and the majority of the marines who serve are as culturally diverse as the world itself. He has also shown me that not all US marines are trigger happy "douche bags."

How on earth did he make it into the US Military? Was he the one who ticked all the ethnic boxes needed for equality? Was he hired on his well-deserved merit? Or was he a sign that the US is not as racist as those of us outside of the US believe it is, and is finally accepting the diverse nature of its citizens?

Reading Jake's story, I have cheered him on, declared "YES!" out loud on many occasions, laughed, and been reminded of global events I saw from a very different vantage point, as well been reminded about numerous personal development methods I have been implementing for the last two decades and have taken for granted.

When Jake told me "I want to write a book, it's going to be this," I remember telling him his original ideas were not only a disservice to himself, his family, and his comrades, but not worth either his time or mine. I will never forget the look on his face as long as I live, it was the perfect look of confusion, excitement, fear, and drive all wrapped up in one.

Watching him get present to just how powerful his story is for others, seeing him struggle with sharing some elements of his story and then playing full out, embodying the courage he has shown countless times in his deployments, and his respect and understanding of the Iraqis has been emotional for us both. His mission is as big as his heart. His desire to continue being of service to his country, of honoring his wife and children, his mentors, fallen comrades and his higher self is inspiring. The dedication he has shown in getting this book written, the excitement he has when seeing his vision coming to life is both heart-warming, exciting, and thrilling.

Jake, it has been an honor to serve with you. You have gifted me a very different idea to what it means to be a marine, whilst also confirming why I would hate for my sons to become marines. People like you make the world a better place, and I am proud to call you a brother, not just a client. I hope your readers are as moved by your story and implement your passion, drive, and determination into turning your recipe into their own, with their own flavors and ingredients.

With love,

Dawn

Dawn
Writer, Author, Business Strategist, Leadership Coach, and Publisher, Keynote Speaker, Location-Free Digital Nomad, and Sailor
https://dawnbates.com

GRATITUDE

To my wife Carol and two loving boys Jaden and Maximilian, I am forever grateful. You were, are and continue to remain the driving force of my life. In my deepest depths, you saved me, uplifted my spirit, and gave meaning to life. You are the cause for living life itself.

To my publisher, coach, and editor Dawn Bates, you helped release the shackles of mental confinement that made my dream of becoming an author come true. You gave way to the freedom of judgment and dump of toxic energy which had been a drain on my spirit. I thank you.

To Pete Canalichio and Scott Mackes, for accepting me into the SABM group, guiding me to Dawn and my personal strengths, and serving as mentors along this journey, I'm indebted to you.

To Marc Brightman and the team at Akamai who played a critical role in developing my purpose and mentoring me on my personal strengths, I thank you.

To the *Animals*, mentors, coaches, leaders, bosses, managers, friends, and family that have been an inspiration along the way—I am happy to have you in my life.

To the Marines that hardened my will: Colonel Cook, Lieutenant Colonel Ayers, Lieutenant Colonel Mainz, Lieutenant Colonel Lappe, Lieutenant Colonel Quinn, Major Redding, Major Hickman, and Captain Maze—you're inspirations and the mettle of America.

PREFACE

In coming up with this book, I was thinking of the *name*, constantly. Something that resonated, something powerful, something eye-grabbing. And to be brutally honest, I wanted something that sold.... a lot. Of course, who wouldn't?

I thought of something that had to have numbers in it, because I was always a fan of numbers. I thought they told a story. I even thought they sold better books!

In my naive and elementary journey, I actually thought the name was just as important as the content itself. Particularly, as inspiration, some of my favorite books: *The Seven Spiritual Laws of Success* (Chopra), *The Four Agreements* (Don Miguel Ruiz)—I thought I'd follow their path and publish *The 30 min Transformation*. A combination of something spiritual like *"transformation"* and attune to my love of numbers.

After the wildly successful *The 4-Hour Work Week* by Tim Ferriss, which I've still yet to read, I thought I'd easily be on my way to publishing a world-class self-help book.

It wasn't until halfway through my writing that I realized that if I was to be sincere and connect with you, the reader, I needed to be sincere with myself. I needed to open up and share with you the epiphany and culmination of 20 years of peaks and valleys, ebb and flow, pain and happiness.

I needed to find you and connect with you in a way that you can see the path.

With further inspiration from one of my favorite artists, I came up with *The Recipe: A US MARINE's Mindset for Success*—thanks Kendrick (Lamar[1])!

In making sure I am keeping honest with you and myself, I'd best be sure to tell you exactly what this book is. Not in an ambiguous manner meant to supersede the value of directness, but in a succinct and visceral message.

This book is my culmination of ingredients that will make you successful.

Plain and simple.

Feel free to alter the *Recipe*, change the ingredients, add in your own spice and garnish—but make no mistake, this is the path. Not to say there are no others out there, but this is a tried-and-true *Recipe*, that, if followed, will ensure your success.

I'll put to rest, immediately, this is not some book on war stories. Any crazed reader looking to find out about death and destruction inflicted by our beloved Corps, please go somewhere else.

For the swarm of hungry and creative readers, who in passing by, were searching for a book about meaning, purpose, identity—this is a story of failures and grit. To those who, after reading, do not put their own personal *Recipe* to use, I wish you luck navigating this lonely world.

For the lost cause of souls wandering this earth, aimlessly looking for your meaning, I hope you enjoy—I wish you the best. If, after walking away from your own dreams of success and accomplishment, are not utterly motivated to gather your ingredients, get back on your path, and make something magical with this time alive, I don't know how else to help you.

If you're of a closed and fixed mindset, I'm sorry *The Recipe* won't serve as your mechanism for change.

I've always been a fan of apologies; I feel they were the best way to move on with something. Say it and go back on to your merry day without a lost thought of the past transpiration. They are the ability to make mistakes and go forward without a care in the world. They bridged the gap from past aggressions to the future. They were a transcendence tool.

Other folks, especially those power-crazed alphas, God love them, probably believe apologetic verses were used by the weak and *enslaved*. In fact, I can recall of instances in a past life where these exact types would tell me "don't apologize," as if they were saving me from some ill-conceived notion that I was not empowered. I wish you well.

To those lost souls I'd mentioned, this one's for you.

In service to your greatness,
Jake

---

1. Kendrick Lamar is an American rapper born in Compton, CA. He's a prolific artist who's partnered with known producer Dr. Dre on Grammy Award winning album *DAMN*.

INTRODUCTION TO "THE STRUGGLE"

For anyone who's had to weather the storm of financial ruin, personal loss, humiliation, despair, melancholy, I can attest, it's a cold, lonely, and treacherous ordeal. You're a helpless victim to the winds and currents. It is a Struggle of lostness and confusion: no direction, no purpose. Trying to find yourself, head down, clutching any solid, sturdy item. Trying to navigate, foolishly, as you convince yourself you have some control, only to be relentlessly rocked. After the struggle, or perhaps in a brief moment of consciousness as the eye of the storm is passing over, you may get a moment of clarity, briefly. You often find yourself wondering just how you came to be in this exact spot. Was it a series of mistakes, one by one, you somehow missed? Or was it a gaff of epic proportions, a swing and a miss on life's grand stage? The ultimate gamble, an all-in bet you lost. Were you wronged somehow? No, maybe just plain stupid. Maybe you'd pushed the envelope just a little too much and this is the repercussions of years of failed planning. Most likely, it's some combination of everything. There's one thing for sure: if not learned, it will be repeated.

Welcome to the Struggle.

Like the survivor of any traumatic event, you start to take

inventory. Piece together the puzzle of chaos you just saw yourself through. You slow down life a bit and rethink a lot more cautiously. Most importantly, you fanatically obsess over your missteps along the way. Like a slow-motion reel on constant repeat, you see your failures plain as day. This inevitably will strengthen your resolve and decide this will not happen again. Not to you. Determined, you make some vows, then changes, then implement new habits along the way. You rebuild. Like a broken bone, growing stronger after its healed—time will heal your ruin. Planning and execution will become your friends and allies, preparing you for the next unknown. You'll want to be shielded, have exit routes, multiple avenues. Your determination and grit will be heightened. Your resolution will be calloused; and then, you'll be ready for the hard work ahead of ensuring you're not in this position again.

Don't be a victim!

Victimhood is the fastest growing career field in America, and around the world.

We are unfortunately experiencing a culture where the ability to be offended is so rampant, it shuts down growth, creativity, and positivity. Cancel Culture—as we call it. The evolution from *Political Correctness* to a society where the ability to fall victim to the words of your fellow brethren is sickening. It is also unfortunately growing. Like the spreading of a wildfire of destruction on your inner peace.

Everyone has an opinion, and more importantly, everyone is entitled to an opinion. Your inability to cope and process the opinion of another is a direct reflection on your maturity and consciousness taking hold. It is your prefrontal cortex trying to control. It is your EGO taking hold and convincing yourself that your perceived notion of control has been challenged and now you thus resort to a defensive state. This defense is in nature if your victimhood is in full swing.

My *struggle* started in summer of 2011 when I was pulled over for a DUI in Hollywood on a Friday night. Booked and brought in around midnight, I blew a .09% (the California legal limit is .08%). .01%, that's all it took to ignite off a series of unfortunate events from that evening forward. I was booked and eventually would go on to spend a weekend in county jail, conduct quite unfit of a US military officer. I would leave the Marines the following year in 2012 with a triple adverse fitness report. (For the non-military folks, this means a Commanding General had to review my file, and ultimately sign off to agree on my level of substandard performance. Since it was a triple, that's 3x the review).

After a decade plus of service and two combat deployments, I was left a broken and broke 30-year-old, one who now had to weather the civilian work force. With legal fees incurred, I'd squandered a decade of military pay, with no assets to my name.

Twelve years in the military takes a toll on the body. Suffering from several dislocated shoulders, gastrointestinal diagnosis, and an arthritic knee. I would have to endure as a "healthy" individual with this banged-up body.

By the end of 2013, the business I'd started with my best friend from high school, Josh, was in ruin and I'd have to subsequently walk away six months after opening our doors.

By March 2014, I'd go on to lose the house I bought after my first deployment and was now a repeat visitor (2x) of Alcoholics Anonymous (AA).

Shortly after, I'd go on to sign my bankruptcy discharge papers in the Superior Court of Oakland, California by spring of 2014. Right around here was my eye of the storm moment. That full-fledged acknowledgement of how poor your previous decisions had been. Most people think bankruptcy is the bottom, where the struggle starts. In fact, at that exact moment in time, with my first-born son just turning five months of age, it was my first glimpse of sunlight. It's the relief. This was my turnaround moment.

It would take me several years to finally evade to navigate this storm. However, the downfall gave me the foundation to rebuild and re-plan for my turnaround story. The bankruptcy lifted a great weight off my shoulders and provided my family the ability to turn our situation around, with focused intent. Like an anchor, it gave me stability to go up from there.

As I left the Marines and, in a way, left myself. I lost my identity. I had lost total control. It was a downward spiral. Familiar to all who've seen it before, I can share with you my emotions of what it's like to hit rock bottom. It looks like someone who's actually stopped caring. Someone, with really no motivation, no will or intent at all—other than to damage their life. No direction! The times you learn the most are when you're at your lowest point. The struggles of life, and setbacks we endure as we navigate our own personal course, are only made more difficult when we don't have a destination.

A single event would be root cause enough to turn your ship around. Somehow, my aforementioned ability to push the envelope never seemed enough. All of the previously listed setbacks, which is exactly what they are: a momentary stop in progress, would cause most to tell a different story. Hide their failures, their misgivings. Highlight only their successes and accolades, as if life is a straightforward escalator to prosperity. I highlight my adversities to share the pains we all have to endure. To give anyone who's lost hope, in doubt, looking for trouble or assistance, this helping hand in life.

Midway through completion, my publisher Dawn Bates (thank you so much!) once again asked me why I was writing this book? After several rounds of bullshit answers, it was not to tell a story, it was to help anyone else in *the Struggle*. We all go through it, we've all been there, we've all hit tilt, we've all fucked up. The world has an amazing way of making everyone other than yourself look like they're perfect. Just the opposite. We're all fuckups in our own beautiful and unique way. My pain might be your pleasure and the exact opposite the very next day. We make mistakes, we dig holes, we hurt others, and then we go on with life. If you're in any sort of depressed, demeaned or otherwise dampened position in life, this is why I wrote this book —for you.

I give to you *The Recipe*, which is my journey through childhood diversity, graduation from the United States Naval Academy, through two combat deployments as a Marine Corps Officer, my struggles through loss of identity after the military and finally my growth through the corporate ladder in various technology companies. *The Recipe* can and will serve as your guidebook for you to navigate life towards the pursuit of a healthy, meaningful, and purpose-driven lifestyle.

Throughout my personal triumph and struggles, I'll expose how I came aware of the power of my subconscious and will give you the keys to unlock it for your own benefit. I write this story for you. For your encouragement of success because, if you're not keenly aware, life's a bitch, and it will only stay that way until you pick yourself up and take it back. Piece by piece. Like the chaos puzzle you put together during the eye of the struggle, my hope for you is you plan a destined life of purpose. I hope for you to paint a picture of the life you want to live. *The Recipe* will help you get there. It will be your greatest asset in this pursuit. *The Recipe* is my saving grace. I know it will be yours too.

I pieced together *The Recipe* through years of reading, writing, and repetition. Each iteration of my personal *Recipe* serves as a test bed for the individual ingredient's success or failure. Each ingredient hypothesized and tested and ensured for success in creating your own personal *Recipe*. Through multiple executive-level leadership programs in my corporate profession, through relearning my instruction serving in a Marine Infantry Battalion and my quest through the Academy—the culmination of my life's work is presented to you in the story to help you achieve more.

To get what you want out of life.

To live with purpose.

After going through my Struggle, I was on a quest for learning and knowledge. I turned to the place where for several millennia we've passed down the history of our world: reading. With each book, each lesson, I would try and test, eventually starting to form an ingredient. The main ingredients I came across through constant, nonstop reading and seeking of knowledge. After the Struggle, every individual I meet, senior or subordinate, I treat as a mentor. Every situation I've progressed from has been the opportunity for learning and growth. Every setback is now an experience. Every door closed, is a new opportunity forming down the road. *The Recipe* came together through consistent testing of daily practice and iteration. The proof, through application in daily life to get what you want. The main ingredient of the *Recipe* is to help you uncover your true want in life and provide you with the means to achieve it. Whether you need guidance, direction, console, help—it will serve as your blessing in life. For those, still searching for their true WANT in life, it will help you uncover your destiny. For those that are lost, this will find and save you, *if you allow it to*.

After daily use and practical application of your *Recipe*, you'll uncover the secret of success: to complete what you plan. You'll leverage your greatest untapped resource, your subconscious. Your machinations will eventually become reality. Your plans for life will be formulated, created, and then executed. You'll become an inspiration to yourself and those around you for executing your life on your terms. The adversities of your past will now serve as a battle hardening of your new distinguishment.

When you're at the bottom, there really is one trajectory: up. We've all had to endure adversity in this world. Get used to it! Some, unfortunately, more than others, and that's okay. You will discover life will deliver as much as you can take. It's up to you to decide when you've had enough. For everyone who's had enough, and needs help in weathering their struggle, *The Recipe* is here to guide you. Give you the ingredients you need to take back your life. It's the key to living a purposeful life. A *Recipe* for success, but more importantly a *Recipe* for life. A guidebook to help you achieve and attain any goal, any want you desire.

We're all chasing something in life: title, rank, promotion, accolades, companionship, or we're not chasing anything at all. If you're not, then you need to be. However, you need to decide, need to conclude what that is for you, I hope this story helps you find your way to a chase, because stagnation is the precursor to death. Life is a collection of experiences that allow us to tell our story with the time we have on this earth. The money, the fame, the recognition, they dissipate. It's all gone when it's over. The experiences stay, they tell your story. What did you do with your time on this earth? What did you experience?

PROLOGUE

The beginning: Growing up, I always wanted ...

Growing up I always knew I wanted more. I dreamt big. I spoke big. I wanted to covet and control and own a mass amount of things. My eyes, hungry as they were, were even more emboldened by this notion that I actually thought I was better than my current standing. As if I was born to achieve and do more, because of some unknown particular gift. That the truest Natural Law, all men are created equal, almost didn't apply to me. Not that I was special. Only that equal men and women, in my mind, would only achieve average things in life. Thus, if you wanted to succeed, to elevate, you had to view yourself as more. Not as more above others, but you only had to want more. I saw myself not just as any equal, nor as some supreme being, rather a curious and hungry child of God with an unquenchable thirst. By no means superior, just not content. Never content. That thirst, to be determined, would be both my curse and my power later in life. It can be yours too. The yin and yang that drive many men/women to achieve great things and punish themselves with equal severity. The curse of "more" is perhaps the most punishing of all, for it is unending. The "not enough", the "I want more" group of people in this world have an insatiable appetite that is only counted as a blessing when used appropriately. I hadn't become consciously aware, until recently, that this thirst was a great shared purpose of many of my Marine brethren. This is the root of any and all children and young adults who aspire to become Marines. A thirst.

Born a quasi-second generation American, which in itself is just as ambiguous as my ethnic diversity, never seemed a difficult steppingstone for me to accept. None more than what I imagine any kid raised in the Xennial generation (born 1977–1985). In fact, our generation is so ambiguous, we don't particularly associate it with a particular Generation "letter" moniker at all. Not a true Millennial, we were some bastardized version of a Gen X and Millennial, thus we'd been aptly titled a *Xennial*. What else better to describe this time period really? So, caught in between the birth of the internet age and the mobile-first generation, we started out a confused demographic cohort and my cultural diversity only seemed to aid this ambiguity. Like many of the immigrants who've ever been asked this question "where are you from?", replying with "California" was always followed on with an even more inconsiderate and equally intolerant question "no, where are you really from?" Particularly, for children to receive this line of questioning, ambiguity is the only way to describe my background.

My mother came to Los Angeles at 20 years old, from Tandag, Philippines. Located in the southern region of the archipelago, it's probably best described as your typical fishing town. As any first-generation Asian woman starting life in a new country, it was hard for her to relate to raising two kids in southern California. This also meant we weren't raised as traditional American kids at that time, which made our relationship distant. Her genetics themselves were as confused as could be as well. Her grandfather was an American *boy* raised in Nebraska who'd found himself in the middle of the Spanish-American War in the early 1900s. He somehow landed in the Philippines fighting the Spanish in pursuit of American interests. As beautiful as I can imagine Nebraska to be, during the winter, he somehow found an affinity and love for the Philippines. So, what better way to settle a war, than to return to the battle land, marry a local Filipina girl and start a family. This turned out to be quite an amazing benefit to their grandchildren, my mother and her mix of 13 brothers and sisters, as luck would have it, they were all born US citizens. Something which, in the times that surround 2021 and the lack of foreign travel, proves to be an amazing inheritance. It is also the first trace our family can recollect to military service.

My father, your traditional patriarch, whose background grows even more complex, had as many identity issues with culture as one probably could have. His father, my grandfather, an Afro-Puerto Rican, had fled Puerto Rico after World War II and found himself stationed as a sergeant in the US Air Force in the 50s. Many stories surrounded my grandfather's leaving of Puerto Rico, but both memory and intrigue leave me with the worst: he had a dramatic scar diagonally across his back. My best recollection, from the single time my father told me the story, was that the police chased him off a bridge as a thief and with a final attempt to capture him slashed their sword in a final blow which inevitably left a permanent scar across his back. I never saw the scar to confirm for myself. Of course, with an imagination as great as my thirst, I love to fill in the rest: that he had a dramatic fall into the blue Gulf Ocean, washed up ashore, and set out to embark on a new life in America. With an exhaustion of relief and nowhere to turn, what better salvation than the US military complex to start life anew. He went on to lie about his age, forge his signature, then enlisted in the US military and found himself a proud Airmen in Southern California. Where truth turns to lie, I'm in the dark, but what I do know is he gave up his father's surname, *Rodriguez*. In Puerto Rico, you have your given name, your father's surname, then your mother's surname. Backwards, I know. However, Osvaldo Rodriguez Cosme Sr, upon entering the US military, out of hatred for his father and upbringing, he kept his mother's maiden name: *Cosme*.

So, to make the identity melting pot of my heritage even more fulfilling, my last name, of French ancestral roots *Cosme*, was actually the maiden name given to my Afro-Puerto Rican grandfather; passed down to my father, self, and now my two children. The stories that surround a French surname in Puerto Rico can only guide the imagination of another story yet to be discovered. My grandmother's (father's mother) heritage equally as distorted, of both Mexican American (San Jose del Cabo, Mexico) and Native American descent (Papago Indian, Arizona), was the culmination of my melting pot, my *Recipe*. No better way to describe my combined ethnicities other than my DNA report: 57% East Asian and Native American (includes: 38% Filipino and Austronesian, 3% Chinese, 16% Native American), 31% European (includes: 28% Spanish and Portuguese, 3% British and Irish), 7% Sub-Saharan Africa (includes: Senegambian, Guinean, Ghanaian, Liberian, Sierra Leonean, and Congolese), 3% West Asian and North African (includes: Arab, Egypt, Levantine)—*thank you 23andme!* (I'd like to take this opportunity to challenge anyone with a more diverse DNA report!)

My family, so varying in its ancestral background, none of us actually resembled each other. My father, stout and heavy set, with a dark brown complexion, mostly mirrored his Hispanic background, but you'd be hard pressed to guess he was Puerto Rican, Mexican, and Native American. My mother, very thin, somewhat tall for a Filipina native, had an incredibly light complexion which shouldn't be surprising at all considering her actual American (Nebraska) roots. You'd think of growing up on an island in the South Pacific for your formative years, you'd have somewhat of a tan? Then my brother, Javier, who is one year my senior, perhaps looked the most Hispanic of all. He had my father's stocky build and my mother's lighted skin tone. Now me, the tall (for a half-Filipino boy), dark-skinned hybrid with an Indian-humped nose, pouty lips, curly hair, and squinty eyes. Everyone as a kid growing up said I looked like my mom. I don't know how as our tints were so vastly distant. Growing up, our family portraits and family reunions made for not only the best food, but the outside perplexment of our backgrounds.

This is where I start, this is where my family came from. Every kid is raised asking about their history, their family, where they're from and how they came to be. This is everyone's first *Recipe*: their background and their roots. For me, this was also the root of both lostness and determination when growing up.

What better place do we find adversity than the adverse nature of not being able to identify as a youth? This is hard for any child of any age, not being able to fit in and find your tribe.

This is the foundation of all future adverse positions: confusion, and the inability to identify. With this inability, what better place to start your journey than to go out and create one?

Build one of your own.

Could a melting pot be any more complex in background, nature, history, culture, diversity than the one I provided? With America, the great melting pot, which we have claimed homage, is my background. I don't see myself as anything but American because I am the living embodiment of the melting pot. This melting pot is my *Recipe*, and we all have our own to make.

I will show you mine.

I will guide you through my path in the hope and faith you will make your own *Recipe*.

You'll guide yourself to success.

So here we go!

ONE

HOW IT STARTED

Race in the 1980s–1990s was more than just a circle on your job or school application. It was what defined you. It defined your culture, your identity, what you ate, what God you prayed to, who you associated with, and possibly your overall standing in life.

Pomona, CA in the late 1980s–mid 1990s was the homicide capital of Los Angeles County for a moment. It was the wild west of gang warfare. A place where African Americans clashed with each other and with Latino gangs. It was far enough from Los Angeles that it was often forgotten about. The east border city which separated Los Angeles County from San Bernardino County, and like any border city, it was the borderlands of lawlessness we think of in modern day. A highly trafficked trade route for drugs, smuggling, prostitution, and despot activity.

My father did his best to shield us as a family from any and all of this. This meant he was very disciplined, stern, and protective. This also meant I was not allowed out much, didn't get to do many activities, and basically left with the front yard as my playground and imagination as my friend. I wouldn't go as far to say he was overprotective, but there was definitely an extreme caution for how far outside my street I could venture. Thus, limited to the cul-de-sac corner of pavement known as Torino Place growing up, this was my stomping ground for my formative childhood years.

Growing up, we always played outside. Everyone knew each other and the neighbors, although not close, were also not against each other. This is all my brother, and I would do growing up, play on this damn pavement, every day. No park, no field, no league sports, just the concrete. Baseball, mostly pickle (a game of two catchers and two bases, tossing back and forth where runners wait for someone to miss then sprint to the other base), football, and bike riding. Thankfully, we had my neighbor Charles, a newly married late twenties–early thirties barber who'd serve as our mentor in these games. With no kids of his own, he was always out there with us. He taught us everything about playing outside. Six foot, jacked, light skinned African American (think of a mix between Will Smith and Ice Cube), he had a lowrider truck and would always cut our hair in his garage, at a discount too! He really would serve as an inspirational figure in my childhood.

Charles hosted a family party growing up and I recollect the time everyone was drinking (alcohol), and I asked him why no beer was in his hand. It was the first time I heard the world "alcoholic." He went on to explain that as an ex-alcoholic he didn't drink anymore. This didn't mean much at the time, but something that stuck with me throughout the years was that people must be forced to give up this toxic consumption. This also meant he found homage in activity, specifically karate. More than a black belt, to what degree I don't know, he'd often compete, and win! He would take us to some of his karate tournaments and to my amazement, I'd watch him beat the shit out of people. To the degree he was deducted points on several occasions for being too aggressive. Imagine settling for second place because you were overpowering your competitor during a martial arts match!

Given these surroundings, my brother and I listened to rap growing up. In fact, it was all we listened to. When Dr. Dre[1] came out with his masterpiece, *the Chronic*, it was the first CD I ever bought.

Growing up with ill means meant you only listened to the radio and this single CD, on repeat. Probably not the best choice for a 10-year-old at the time, but it was the foundation for our time. This also meant we were bored a lot. One CD and catch in the front yard, very limited options compared with the youth of this generation. So, we actually would do our homework and study. I could never have the attention span to understand what I was reading; so, I would always stare off in imagination. I did however read aloud particularly well, just with little afterward comprehension. Being left with good study habits and verbal dialogue, people and teachers would reward A's and often think I was smart… or at least a smart ass. Lacking the ability of thorough comprehension, I was nothing more than a brown kid who knew at an early age how to pronounce well in a class with half the population as bilingual. Hardly a savant.

These years, formative and fun to an extent, were all also very boring. This served any kid with an over imagination and verbal diarrhea poorly, it meant I would always be in trouble. Mostly, for lying, occasionally for stealing, the infrequent cheating combined with the consistent backtalk certainly didn't help along the way nor my inability to thoroughly comprehend. It just meant I'd talk without thinking, thus making any bad situation worse. With two disciplinarians as parents, I was grounded (put on restriction) quite frequently. The "groundings" meant you were restricted to your room. No phone, TV, radio, etc., just room and bed and time. This would serve profoundly for developing a need down the line to think of escape. In fact, I'd be in so much trouble so often, my parents used to think there was something wrong with me and pondered seeking professional help. Thankfully, their means were limited, and this basically meant no money was ever spent on development.

Coming from a long lineage of military service, dating back to the early 1900s, escape meant I would more than likely end up joining a branch as well. My father would wake up my brother and I every morning on the weekends to the same tune played during reveille while he was in boot camp. This abrupt awakening would then lead to breakfast, chores, and yard work. Not only would we service our yard, our first job was maintaining the neighbors as well. For the mightily sum of $3/each, my brother and I grew up working every weekend. I'm sure there was a ton of development attributed to starting work at such an early age and the concept of knowing what a "buck" was worth. However, I will never subject my children to labor at such an early age. Take this for what it's worth. The value of discipline, commitment, and hard work can equally be instilled through sports on the field, rather putting a 9–10-year-old through manual labor. After having children of my own, I realized their minds, like sponges, soak. Teaching them to push a lawn mower is hardly the *Recipe* I would want for mine.

Finishing up 6th grade, rounding out our time in elementary school at 11 years of age, we were fortunate that our parents did care for a higher education. As much as you can shield a young child through their youngster years, maintaining a keen eye over a preteen and teenager would be much more difficult. Our parents made an easy and inconvenient decision to send us to school in the neighboring and more ritzy/affluent city, Diamond Bar. This particular city will come into play much later on as well, luck would have it my future wife would also be a Diamond Bar native.

In the 7th grade, upon assignment of a book report, I found myself in our Lorbeer Junior High school library scourging around. Whether fate or familiarity found me, I came across a book dedicated to the *United States Naval Academy*. Mostly a picture book with limited descriptions, ideally leveraged to showcase the Brigade of Midshipmen in uniform, of course, sports facilities, and ideal location on the bank of the Severn River. Founded in 1945 in Annapolis, Maryland; the pre-civil war institution was and still remains the steadfast competition to West Point (Army). Upon first sight, I was mesmerized by the building architecture, the beautiful state of Maryland and this proving ground of our nation's collegiate adults. Having come from a strong military family it seemed normal that I was consistently bombarded with notions of also being of service in the military after high school. The Academy offered perhaps the greatest escape: service, college, and the unknown. From there forward, this institution would serve as my *Recipe*. Everything I would do from 7th–12th grade would be in hopes of receiving an appointment to the *Academy*.

Upon standing in front of that 7th grade class for delivery of my book report, a witty bunch of pubescent youths, (like most things in my life) I bombed it on the first attempt. My teacher, entirely not pleased with my delivery, asked for a repeat. She refused to give me a grade and I was forced for a repeat recital to this class. Second time, like a charm, was a passing grade, but my first step towards Academy indoctrination ended in a fail. A life-daunting process, I'd continue to fail, repeat, then pass. This was the first recollection I have of a failure in pursuit of a goal. Certainly not the last, it would be a continuous cycle for the rest of my life.

From 7th grade forward, everything I strived to achieve in academic life would be in preparation of applying to the Academy. Most importantly, the book I found and the several in class presentations would imprint this institution into my mind. This was the first glimpse of something I wanted, something major in my life I would pursue. It would go on to consume my subconscious and impregnate my mind. At night I would pray, think, and dream of the Midshipmen, the green grounds, and life inside this 150+ year old stone dormitory, the largest in the United States. At that time, 1995, with no computer or internet in the house, these few pictures I had of the Academy would be enough to channel this want into my subconscious. **This was the first want I had in life**. Not knowing whether I would soon achieve it or not, I was left with a constant and repetitive prayer to see it to fruition.

Having this want was also the first formulation of *The Recipe*. The imprint of images into my mind, staying up at night and ruminating about this institution. It would consume my prayers and thoughts, in a dark room, with no phone, no computer, no TV, this was my thought. By fate or luck, it would serve to keep me company on a nightly basis.

From grades 7–12, those incredibly formative nights saw the ushering of my teenage years.

After 7th grade, my family would decide to move to a nicer yet remote city, east past the borders of Los Angeles County to a multicolored, tract house in the town of Rancho Cucamonga. Definitely not the Kansas I was used to. It would be my stomping grounds for the next few teenage years.

My grades remained steady, mostly A's, and yet I would continue getting into trouble and still have a longing for fitting in. Not going to the elementary or middle school prior meant that high school was a fresh start with no friends. This also meant the exploration of clubs and sports. All in the attempt to ensure I had a robust resume for the Academy after graduation, I would try everything. Junior Reserve Officer Training Corps (JROTC[2]), Drill Team, Class Senate, Pacific Islander Club, etc. not just for exposure, I was also looking for the right place to fit in. My people and my tribe to accompany me through these years. For sports, I did wrestling and tennis. With not much success in either, I would end up quitting everything by my senior year.

By the time I was 14, I went from weekends of yard work to a busboy gig in a Mexican restaurant, *Socorro's*. School and sports during the week, cleaning tables on the weekends, this was my life up until 17. Thankfully, working gave me money I didn't have to ask my parents for, and it also meant I could drive once I turned 16. (In fact, my parents even got me a beater Honda Civic as my first car, which I would go on to crash several months later.) Armed with mobility and money (a deadly combination for any teenager), the ability for escape would finally be here. My escape eventually found itself in raving. The close companion of late-night warehouse parties is, yes, drugs. Chiefly, *ecstasy*. (aka X, XTC, molly, MDMA, E, candy). There really is no shortage of nicknames for this potent pill; it's a miracle worker.

[*side bar:* I would like to thoroughly take this time to vehemently state that I do not condone the use of narcotics by minors. However, I'd be remiss to not highlight this very formative time period in my life. I'm sure a lostness and confusion of many teenage wonder years are spent in experimentation.]

Your first "*roll*" as they call it, about 30–45 minutes after taking the magic pill is unforgettable. A feeling of warmth and euphoria consumes you. The next four to eight hours are of the highest intensity state you'll ever experience. It's pure sensory overload. It's a pleasure to an unknown degree. You won't be hooked like some degenerate crack addict (not passing judgment here by any means) fiending the streets at night. You will however remember this first particular sensorics awareness with profound blithe. It's as if every cell in your body is for the very first time working in pure harmonic perfection.

My future lifelong friends, Andrew and Eddy would accompany throughout this transitory period during our last and final year in high school. The weekends, partying, the experiences, the upheaval we raised, it was the best year of my life. This lostness I had, this wandering, this melancholy would be at an end. We would go on to get our first girlfriends together, lose our virginity at similar times, rave (more), crash cars, prom / dances, dyed hair, baggy clothes. It was 1999, heading into 2000 as college seniors and an amazing time to be alive. It would be my last year before leaving for the military school and it was unforgettable. Drugs and girls / weed and women—not a care in the world and no fucks given!

Looking back, there really is no better way to have finished that last year in Rancho Cucamonga. Andrew and Eddy still remain friends to this day. In fact, I would go on to meet my future wife (Carol) through Andrew and our children now play together on birthdays. Unaware of the grueling road ahead, I'm overwhelmed with joy that I was afforded this special time in life before what lay ahead. There's nothing I would change about the conclusion of my high school life.

———————————————

1. Andre Young, also known as Dr. Dre, is an American rapper and producer, best known for his breakout album *The Chronic*. Born and raised in Compton, CA, he's an original member of N.W.A. and former partner with Death Row Records.
2. JROTC: Junior Reserve Officer Training Corps is a high school (secondary school) program throughout the United States to teach, train, and inform students of military history, traditions, and decorum.

TWO
PREP SCHOOL

By all means an average student, below average athlete, and run of the mill Xennial from suburbia. The only thing I had different was this thought I implanted of the Academy into my mind seven years prior. I spoke to the gods above about this manifestation every night. Finishing up senior year, I was denied from West Point, the Air Force Academy, and UCLA (I didn't bother with USC? Why? My family had no way of paying for it). The rejections came in so quickly I do wonder if they actually had time to review the full application. Looking back, it made sense these denials were flowing, it was not meant to be. Those schools would not be the future I was destined for. They were not what I wanted and not the dreams of my mind. For seven plus years, my prayers gave energy to the Naval Academy, therefore this would be path and course in life.

    Like any destination, it also didn't come easy. I failed on my first application attempt. No surprise there, failing was now becoming commonplace in life. I unfortunately was not granted a direct appointment to the Academy, instead I was afforded the opportunity to spend a year at preparatory school, and after successful completion of studies and sports, I'd be granted an appointment to the class of

2005 at the United States Naval Academy (USNA). This would be a mix of college and military purgatory. Grind it out for a year and if you make it through the other side, we let you in our pearly gates.

The prep school assigned to me: Naval Academy Prep School (NAPS) in Newport, Rhode Island. I never went for a school visit and did not have much information on what the year entailed. On July 20, 2020, with parents at my side, I flew cross country to this tiny "island" for what would be a mock boot camp "indoctrination" (indoc) before the school semester started. The first day of our three-week indoc, I woke up screaming. My bunk mates, a Marine Lance Corporal and stout Greek (Patrick Drosinos) awoke in amazement to this whining child lost in his place.

I had no idea what I was in for. Just the weekend prior, I was at a rave in Downtown Los Angeles. No more than seven days later, I found myself in a military barracks in Rhode Island, crammed with two unknown individuals and a cadre of instructors outside my hatch banging metal instruments at 5am. Having spent the past year quite literally in "dick off" mode, I was in for a rude awakening. Not a single ounce of energy my senior year was spent on preparation for this school nor the indoc. I was rolling and puffing menthols all summer in a last-ditch hoorah to not grow up. Now, I found myself, middle of summer, in a far-off state in this pickle.

Those next three weeks would be the most difficult of my young adulthood. Not due to any particular physical or mental activity; rather, I was out of place. I was lost again. Having spent sixteen years looking for meaning and then finding it, my senior year was now at an end. I had to start over again. You see, when you go to the Academy, you owe (at a minimum) five years of military service afterwards. So, this meant, one year of prep school, four years at the Academy and five years of post-military officership service. Coming to terms with accepting an appointment to the Academy and subsequent service would mean my next decade would be accounted for. My journey in life would be decided by this commitment. This is quite the coming to terms for a 17-year old whose only venture outside of CA was

Tijuana and Rosarita beach, Mexico. Give up my next decade of life and venture into the unknown or quit and go back to the nefarious life of a teenage dirtbag?

Those three weeks eventually passed, I finished NAPS indoctrination and went on to somehow make it through the next ten months. That year in Newport was my coming of age. I turned 18, could officially purchase tobacco (smokes and dip), and officially be out past 10pm—yay! Like many things at prep school, I needed that year to figure myself out. To come to age with who I am. I also did not lose my ability to somehow always find and attract trouble.

My roommate (Andres Juarez, Andy) grew to be close friends. Both fans of movie quotes and Arnold Schwarzenegger, he was a mighty Texan and all-around great guy. We still stay in touch to this day and after two decades of friendship will still quote the same movies, which also entail a perfect recital of *Half Baked*. In fact, we can probably have a full-on conversation with only movie quotes, in perfect detail to catch up. Andy and I would go on to befriend Adriel Morgan (Kalamazoo, MI), Brandon Alamo (Miami, FL), Mike Brock (Chicago, IL), and Joe Johnson (Coast Guard) as our group of friends during that time at NAPS. We even had a corny nickname "Mod Squad" to solidify our friendship. This also meant I had company for any future shenanigans we'd uncover.

That Halloween of 2000, the squad, my Platoon mates and I decided it would indeed be a fantastic idea to "egg" the communal bathroom and shower stalls of our sister platoon. Not an idea born out of boredom, it was retribution. Being in 2nd Platoon, several of our female candidates carved and lit a pumpkin for the weekend. Placed upon a stool for our area of the bricked dorms, it was a nice homage to real life. The dirty bastards in 1st Platoon thought it a wily idea to steal said pumpkin and trash it across our hall. I can't recall their motivation for starting this heinous act, but I do know, they started it.

Armed with six dozen eggs, that Friday night as the entire company (all three other platoons) went to watch a Halloween movie in the gymnasium—we snuck out under the guise of a bathroom break and went to town like aspiring pitchers at AAA tryouts demolishing the joint washing facility (aka head—bathroom). As if 72 eggs were not enough, they were soon followed by toilet paper and trash dispensed across the floor. Mission complete! This was surely an admirable retribution to someone stealing our pumpkin. Much satisfied in our work, we returned to watch the same movie, with an uncontrollable smirk across our faces. The look one has when thinking, *they'll never know it was us*.

An unknown, wary candidate from the sister platoon (1st Platoon), needing a bathroom break, soon discovered their single restroom facility demolished. This stranger, unaware of what to do tells their friend, then another. As we began to notice, more and more classmates started getting up from the movie to check the mess enthralled upon their restroom and shower stalls. We stayed focused and resolute in our smirks in order to not give up our guilt. You never want to let on that the jig is up.

The aftermath which ensued was riveting. In what seemed like the food fight from *Animal House*, 1st Platoon immediately retaliated in kind by destroying our living quarters, soon followed by a bomb rush in our seated positions at the movie theatre. The unrest which arose would be aptly referred to as a "riot" in our punishment and hearings.

Following the event, we received maximum restriction and demerits. Thankfully saved from expulsion, we were unable to return home for Thanksgiving and the holidays. Having to explain to your parents that you could not come home for the holidays due to *"inciting a riot"* was hard to deliver and I imagine even harder for them to hear. As well, we had complete confinement to our rooms for the next sixty days. This also meant that any other violation, suspension, punishment would be grounds for expulsion from NAPS and the US Navy and any dreams of the Academy would vanish. I would be walking on eggshells from here on out as we entered 2001.

I ended up finishing prep school and my fellow band of rioters and I made it to the Academy in June of 2001. We would all go on to graduate in May 2005 some several years later. The *Squad* would continue to stay in touch throughout the Academy but after graduation, it would be hard to keep up. Andy and I went on to become Marine Officers, Brandon a Naval Aviator, Mike a Naval Surface Warfare Officer (SWO), and Joe a Coast Guard Officer. Adriel would finish the academy and graduate with us, but due to an injury sustained during boxing was to become a civilian after graduation and pursue his destiny as both a teacher and track coach; no better service I can think of for a man of his leadership and talents.

THREE

THE ACADEMY

The plague of "proper" English

I was never the best, at anything, ever. Always the perennial semi-smart kid who often relied upon getting by with "good enough" rather than a true discipline and dedication to any particular subject. A real smart ass who relied upon answers to come easily, rather than truly learn. Math always seemed to come easiest, maybe because of the years spent studying the multiplication table on the inside of my peach-colored *Pee-Chee* All Season Portfolio folder as a child. (Those of you in the US may recall the bland recycled paper, light-weight folder with 60s style American athletes doing basic running, tennis, basketball, and baseball which could never seem to last more than one semester of abuse). Despite my ability to recall this table and all numerical inhabitants instantly, I somehow opted to take AP (Advanced Placement) English in my Junior (3rd) year of high school. My first "advanced" class in my 11 years of schooling. Unsure why I decided on advanced English instead of sticking to my strengths of math, I clung to my thirst of wanting more and decided, *why not*.

Within the first week, it was evident I had no idea how far behind in "proper" English I truly was. For the past 10 years, the ability to read and regurgitate substance, via any book report, was all that was required to pass American English class. (A real testament to our education). Not only did I pass, apparently it was enough to have placement in an "advanced" class by the time I was ready to graduate formal schooling. What quickly became evident was that any ability to read aloud with a decent contrast of pronunciation and pause was pale in comparison to my complete lack of understanding in basic sentence form and structure. I was terrible. I could hardly tell the difference between various types of nouns (pro, proper, collective…). Further, I had no understanding of basic sentence structure. Who knew you needed both an adjective and a verb? I progressed those next five months throughout the semester in anguish. The class act portrayal which had worked for my entire youth was exposed. The first test of my mental abilities had failed. I finished the semester with a C⁻. In all truth, it was a good ol' fashioned D. The teacher took pity on me. God bless her soul.

My only saving grace that semester was our final extracurricular project. It was left open to any creative project. I decided to write an extension to Edgar Allen Poe's *The Raven*. It was a five pager that, in true Poe dramatic fashion, I read aloud, in a dark, candle lit English room to the students. Most resembling a poetry recital, I actually received some praise for the writing. My merciful teacher, shocked how this flippant, lackey of a student who had failed her all semester was able to deliver a *decent* follow-on performance to an amazing and timeless poetic masterpiece left me with a "you couldn't give me that all semester?" look on her face. No, I couldn't. Perhaps, this was the Hail Mary which turned my D to C, in the end, I don't know. But, in true form, after being behind for months, I wanted to go out with a slam dunk, and this performance elevated my failure to a passing.

I've never taken an advanced class since, but this begrudgingly difficult period gave me the foundation I'd continue to build upon:

I may not know jack shit of our language, but creativity and imagination can always save your ass.

Two years later, after the indoctrination to the Academy, all Midshipmen were required to take placement exams. Not surprising, I was put into remedial English at the Academy, aptly nicknamed *Trucker English*. By no means an insult to the fierce-hearted drivers who power our roadways and keep our international commerce business alive. Like many nicknames at the Academy, you're not entirely sure on their origin or background but you keep the tradition alive. Because tradition is what keeps the institution alive. The best way to think of our sanative standing as a *Trucker* of English was this: people describe things slower to you.

Joking aside, what this story will hopefully expose, no matter how smart you think you are, no matter what accomplishments you've been able to skate through in the past—you won't know your true standing until you've pushed to the next level. Until you find yourself the dumbest in the room surrounded by those with the knowledge you desire, you will always be the dumbest smart ass. Strive to be the dumbest in the room because that means you'll have the opportunity to learn from everyone around you. You'll get better. You'll build. Then, even if you fail for months, maybe you'll come out with a Hail Mary. Maybe if you fail in an entire subject, you'll succeed in one small area. Maybe you'll tell a great story, land a big deal, and every failure of that half year will NOT end in vain.

Let this be a note. Anyone can and will fail when challenged appropriately. It's during this time of test, you'll expose something about yourself. An attribute about yourself may come forth and be drawn out. This will come later and manifest itself into your power.

At NAPS, we competed in NCAA Division III, which basically meant I was bad enough to retain a spot on the wrestling team.

Unfortunately, once you got to the academy, it was a Division I school. All the recruited athletes from NAPS, mostly football, were now competing for Division I spots—the top in the collegiate nation. Not wasting my time, I gave up on wrestling and decided to pursue boxing. Growing up in a household that watched all the great Mexican, Puerto Rican, and African American boxers—I wanted to try this sport for myself. Similar to wrestling, it's a 1:1 sport with a ring instead of a mat. 3 x 3-minute rounds determine the victor. This was the most physically demanding sport I've endured to date. Over the next three years of competition, I would go on to hang up my gloves before senior year with an overall record of: 0-2.

Each year at the academy is marked by a particular rank and also a statue of what rights you're allowed. As a freshman, you're referred to as a plebe[1]. Everyone else, not a plebe, you address as Sir or Ma'am all year. You're also not allowed certain rights to hallways, elevators, stairwells, etc. Further, you're not allowed to walk inside the halls during daylight hours. You're forced to jog or lightly run through the halls, everywhere. To class, to meals (breakfast/lunch/dinner), to studying, everywhere you go inside that massive dormitory is spent running when the sun is up. When inside the hall, running, you're also not allowed outside a main line. You're forced to run in the center, in a line, with only the ability to make sharp 90 degree pivots, no curved turning. Quite lastly, not really a right, more an obligation—while running (everywhere), straight line, middle of the hallway, no turning, on every sharp 90 degree change, you're forced to scream "Go Navy, sir" or "Beat Army, sir"[2] This lasts all year. For a full year, you cannot walk during daylight hours in the world's largest connected dormitory. Any outside visitor that frequents the academy grounds during lunch hour would bear witness to the vocal carnage bellowed by anywhere from 1100–1300 screaming freshman, running in pearly white uniforms screaming "Go Navy Sir … Beat Army Sir"; all of them, like clockwork at the exact same time, every day of the week… for an entire year.

After being a Plebe, life at the Academy was not as terrible as it may seem. The daily schedule, the regimented nature, the same uniform, were all benefits in their own way. They were a reset. Everyone was in their struggle, united together to make it through and graduate. No one's past, family, or previous prestige mattered. No one competed for status. No one had the ability to set their position, ego, or superiority complex ahead of another. This commonality we all shared made it easier to focus. It gives you the time to study and excel in sports. Even athletic competitions had nothing to do with being better than someone. They had to do with being the best version of yourself. In all honesty, it felt like the one place where you did not have to be great at something. Being good enough was surprisingly an excellent position at this institute. **You did not have to put on a front**. You did not have to pretend. It was a privileged time where I never felt judged.

This identity, of not being judged, not having to compare, was stupendous for my growth and identity. My roommate, William Brumley II, aka Bill Junior, whose nickname "BJ" was the best description of any name, was my counterpart in this journey. We befriended each other Plebe year through watching movies on our off time. Then, by reciting movie quotes, daily, hourly, every time possible. It was the best of times.

I had an identity as a Midshipman. I had unity in our struggle through the commonalities we all shared in this institute. I was in peak physical performance. I even had a girlfriend the first two years. The families in the Annapolis area would often "sponsor" midshipmen on the weekends which allowed everyone the chance to visit a local/normal family, soothe in a "house" on any available time off and offer rescue from the walls of the Academy. I'm forever grateful to the Hitt family (Mark, Nancy, Caitlin, and Greg) for being my sponsor family and my saving grace during this time period. We try to stay in touch as much as possible over the years, but being on opposite coasts, it is often difficult to bond).

My academics at the Academy, as noted above with being a *Trucker*, were a struggle. I had to work my ass off just to get C's.

Wherein high school and every grade preceding, I could do work last minute, sometimes on the fly and sneak away with an A, now I was at full mental production struggling to keep a 2.0 GPA. This is the only way to describe the Academy really, school, sports, and hard work. Four years of head-down grinding. With some brief intermissions during summer months, it's a bleak citadel where the only goal is to graduate, by any and all means possible.

Not all bad, there were some really great moments in this locked-up lifestyle. With no option other than to stay active, I was able to experience many things not afforded to your typical collegiate adult. Boating on the Severn River, patrolling the Atlantic Northeast during the summer, jumping out of helicopters, summers spent at jet aviation squadrons, weeks underwater on submarines, and months out at sea on Naval warfare ships. I had exposure to all facets of our Naval military service. Weekend tournaments with the Ultimate Frisbee Team were the best getaways as a midshipman. What better way to escape a US military institution than a full weekend tournament playing frisbee at colleges up and down the tri-state corridor?

Accompanied with my new posse, roommate BJ (real name William Brumley Junior, aka Bill Junior), Trey (Edgar Alverson III), and Braxton Mashburn (Brax) and the amazing refuge and love from an unknown family, the Hitt family, provided me with so many blessings to persevere through the tough times during those four years at Annapolis.

At the age of 21, at the start of my junior (2nd class) year, I was firmly in love with alcohol. It provided a safe haven. A grace for me. I was not running away from anything, yet it provided an escape. The ability to "black out" was an unsurpassed state I would often chase. No pleasure in actually leveraging alcohol to fit social norms. No, it was this state of "not knowing" which I chased after, the waking up in mystery as to what occurred previously. This was the rabbit in my race. I was not running from anything, nothing to feel sorry about, nothing to pity myself on. It was the state that called me. Living in the limbo of conscious and unconscious. A most terrible place. The strength it provided many to "socialize" was not shared upon me. In fact, it provided me the strength to feel okay NOT socializing. Not communicating. It gave me an arena where I could actually do nothing in a crowded environment and feel absolutely "OKAY". I was not in pain; I was not running from anything. In fact, the discovery of this unconscious state gave me something to look forward to. This would be a continuous bane in my future self and also the cause to many, if not all, of my downfalls.

I'd always "tried" beer and alcohol in high school, but with little regard for the taste and an abhorrent gag reflex every time I took a shot, it was never quite my thing. It would definitely become my "thing." Much like the senior year of high school, the final year of the Academy (First Class midshipmen is the title referred to, or *Firstie* for short) was again a tremendous time of life. There is a saying in the Navy, the two best ranks are: Admiral and 1st Class Midshipmen. I've never been an admiral, but I can attest to the life of a Firstie. BJ, Trey, Brax and I would live up that last year to its best. Golf tournaments (BJ and Brax were both collegiate Division I golfers), parties at University of Maryland, downtown Annapolis, Washington DC nightclubs; after four years of isolation from NAPS through now, it was a "blow-off top" kind of year, once again.

The identity I had for these brief, formative, transitional, and amazing four years would come to a halt my senior "First Class" year. Your fourth and final year at the Academy grounds are really amazing. After not having anything for the previous three, the ability to wear civilian clothes on the weekends and own a vehicle were God-like privileges. This last year also provided me the highest anxiety ever felt—with having to make a choice of what I'd do after graduation. What service would I choose: Navy or Marines Corps? What occupational specialty would I pursue?

Having found this miraculous and coincidental book in 7th grade, then going on to pray, dream, and chase the idea of the Academy for my wonder years was coming to an end. The four years at the Academy was a proving ground for my identity to becoming an adult.

What would I do now? I found my mental state in much affliction during this time. My family, having mostly served in the Air Force, would think no higher prestige than becoming a Naval Aviator. Having grown up on *Top Gun* throughout the 80s, this was surely to be my calling. However, in the fall of 2004, our country was in a deep and entrenched battle in both Iraq and Afghanistan. There was a calling I needed to answer. I felt I needed to be on the ground and see what was taking place. I was not chasing warfare nor glory. I was not seeking destruction. I had this overwhelming and underlying feeling that I needed to see, witness, and live firsthand what it would be like in a combat zone in a third-world country. Almost like a news reporter yearning for a story. I needed to live and breathe this state of being in foreign clime and place.

After being rejected (No surprise! Rejection is the story of my life at this point remember?) as a Marine Officer on my first attempt/application in October of 2004, I was hopeful yet sadly disappointed I did not acknowledge my calling earlier in life to be a US Marine. After my second attempt to pursue this life, in November, ahead of Christmas break, I was granted an audience with our Marine selection committee at the Academy and pleaded my case to choose this lifestyle. By December, I was offered an appointment as a 2nd Lieutenant in the United States Marine Corps (USMC) following graduation in 2005.

My family, over Christmas dinner, was in startling disbelief I gave up a guaranteed contract as a Naval Aviator to become an undesignated Marine Ground Officer, during a time of dual wars. They thought this a knee jerk reaction to some bravado. When in fact, just the idea of flying actually seemed quite boring. After you do it once, you're just stuck in a confined environment. For hours.

I would go on to graduate in May 2005, and this identity as a Midshipman was over. My dream since 7th grade, 11 years old, was over. It was accomplished. My next mission would be upon me, to be a Marine Officer during a time of combat. My friends would go on to their respective services and occupational specialties, and I would forge ahead to Quantico, Virginia for the hardest months of my adulthood. A new identity would be bestowed upon me.

Graduation from the Academy, May 2005, was my first pinnacle of life and perhaps my greatest achievement to date. It represented more than a diploma from an institution of great prestige. It represented the unlocking of a great power I'd yet to fully grasp at the time. **The power of your subconscious**. The power to convince your mind anything is possible, put it out in the world and actually have it come to fruition. This is the greatest force in all of the universe. It separates the humans from all other animal species. It's our subconscious. It holds the power of anything you want in its grasp. It marked the end of my childhood dream and the evolution of becoming an adult. I would now be in actual service to my country. Not school, not studying, not some institution where I had to go through studying and sports. Time for the actual test of men and women: leadership.

True to form in all my previous attempts for anything in life, I failed at becoming a Marine my first time around (this is quite the theme of this story). Winter of your *Firstie* year (Nov–Dec 2004) you have to list what you want to do after graduation. There are two branches of service to choose from, Navy or Marine Corps, and several options for each branch.

Naval Officers choose from:

- Surface Warfare Officer (SWO)
- Submarine Officer (SO)
- Aviation Officer (Pilot)
- Naval Flight Officer (NFO)
- Special Warfare Officer (SEALS)

- Special Operations Officer (EOD, Explosive Ordnance Disposal)

Marine Officers have options:

- Ground Officer
- Aviation Officer (Marine Pilot)
- Flight Officer (Marine NFO)

Failing to be a Marine for the first time around, due to a surge in numbers needed for fighting two warfronts in both Afghanistan and Iraq, the Academy was allowed to produce ~40 more officers to send the Marines Corps instead of Naval service. I was fortunately allowed one of these positions. I would not get my first option, Marine Pilot, and would instead be selected for Marine Ground Officer. This meant I would go on to The Basic School (TBS) in Quantico and then select from the ~23 options afforded to Marine (non-pilot) officers.

---

1. Plebe, also see "pleb", the plebeians were the working class, non-aristocratic ordinary citizens of ancient Rome. Without rank or title, they were generally regarded as a tier above slave without the ability to own land.
2. The United States Military Academy at West Point, New York is the Army collegiate military institution. Referred to as "cadets," they play the Navy "midshipmen" in an American football game every year, dating back to 1890. It is America's oldest sports rivalry. In testament to their (Navy) conviction of being a superior institution and military branch, plebes use "Beat Army" as their motto.

FOUR

USMC

Discipline

"**Discipline** is an **instant** and willing **obedience** to all **orders**, respect for authority, self-reliance and teamwork."

This is the only separation from our branch of service versus all US military branches: Army, Navy, Air Force / Space Force, Coast Guard. There's no particular job (occupational specialty), function, nor capability the Marine Corps possesses over the other branches of services. The various roles across specialties in the Marines fall within three groups: Ground Combat, Combat Support, and Aviation Combat. Our ground combat battalions of infantry, tank, artillery, and combat engineer pale in size to the masses which make up the Army. Our combat support units and specialties—logistics, communications, supply, and intelligence—are replicated across all military branches. Aviation combat elements, comprising fixed (attack, fighter, refueling) and rotary (carrier, attack, utility) wing aircraft platforms—are shared across the various branches as well. The sheer existence of the United States Marine Corps is discipline. Most specifically: **instant and willing obedience to all orders**. *Instant and willing*—we carry out orders faster than any unit in the world. Speed. We can inflict American willpower (combat operations) at any place in the world faster than any force in history.

Our basic and officer training duration extends past all branches for the installation of discipline. Our TBS is six months of officer training, Boot Camp is 12 weeks (longer than any indoctrination camp for any service), and our Infantry Officer Course (IOC) is 13 weeks. Ranger school is only ~60 days. The conviction of will, the physical and mental hardening bestowed upon all Marines to make them the most disciplined **takes time**. We give the title of *"United States Marine"* to ensure discipline is maintained well after basic training and occupational specialty. The installation of all of our ethos exists to ensure we stay disciplined.

> *Every Marine a Rifleman.*
> *Once a Marine, Always a Marine.*
> *Semper Fidelis "Always Faithful"*

These mottos exist for continued conviction of discipline well after training is complete. You can think of them as daily affirmations to ensure good order is kept and you don't forget who you are.

The Marines Corps is an identity change. Becoming a Marine changes who you are. How you look, speak, act, carry yourself—you are a changed person. Going through the various training and indoctrinations is not just for molding of the body, but the mind. Changing your identity does not come easy. In fact, it takes the following weeks (as mentioned above) of complete immersion before the mind is convinced you are now someone else. This seeks to separate the Marines from all other branches. If their training is the longest, they go deeper into the subconscious to establish the new identity. Upon full completion, the identity is changed forever.

You are now "Once a Marine, Always a Marine". This motto only holds true for the Marine Corps because their training is not one of instruction, it's of identification.

This was an impactful time for me. Those years as a child feeling lost, then found in my various ways meant I was now someone else, someone different. I almost had to forget my past and fall into this identity of what would be needed to excel as a Marine Officer. This is something everyone must go through as they become a Marine. The Marines give you a way of life, a formula to live by. Inevitably it gives you order out of chaos. The same goes for your personal life. Without a *Recipe*, you'll continuously be in chaos.

The Order

> "Anyone who takes a **life** it is as though he has destroyed the universe and **anyone who saves a life** it is as though he has saved the universe." – Qur'aan

A Marine Corps order imbues with it the constitutional powers, the right and, if necessary, the obligation to take human life, when necessary. And when necessary, to save a human life. Officers are commissioned under the authority of the President and therefore legally bound to give, take, receive, and execute orders. What is an order? An authoritative command. When giving an order, you are commanding. When receiving an order, you are commanded to execute this legally binding, constitutionally upheld directive. An order received by a Marine Commander and disseminated through the various chains of command therefore imbibes all Marines, on each level of the chain, this taste of divinity. Thus, any order then received is made sacred. Its accomplishment is therefore a universal law which must be upheld. The recipients who must see its execution carried out are now in tune with the universe from its receipt until its fulfillment. This wielding of power an order has cannot be more overstated. The discipline of every Marine has been instilled for over 250 years, before the birth of the United States,[1] for the upholding of this clear obligation.

Every time a Marine unit executes on a mission, it's from an order. When you stand duty, you have standing orders. When you march somewhere, it's from an order. Before every live fire exercise, drill, movement, patrol, mission, everything you do comes from an order. When you change duty stations, you receive "orders" to permanently change stations.

An order has a process and a structure. We're not just a band of Spartans running around barking legally binding orders everywhere. The Operation Order (OpOrd)[2] follows the combat order process:

- Begin planning
- Arrange for reconnaissance and coordination
- Make reconnaissance
- Complete plan
- Issue order
- Supervise

From here forward, we'll only focus on the most critical and pertinent area: Issuing order. The OpOrd has a very particular format. It comes in five paragraphs:

1. Situation
2. Mission: Commander's Intent
3. Execution
4. Admin and Logistics
5. Command and Signal

SMEAC [*smee ack*] as an acronym for memory and a short form for the five-paragraph order is the basis for issuing every order to Marines. (Below is the exact definition from the Marine Corps Training Command. I'd be both plagiarizing and doing a disservice to the exact definition of the elements of the order if I was to interpret and reword for this book).

I. Situation: will contain information detailing the specifics and overall status of friendly and enemy forces. It will give you the "lay of the land" to provide the overall demographics of the battlefield.

> A. Enemy forces: subparagraph will provide information concerning their location, size, makeup, weapons, capabilities, and activities. It will detail their all facets, with information available to help you exploit their weakness. It will also provide information regarding their plan of action. Whether they plan to defend or attack. Whether they're entrenched or planning a withdraw.
> B. Friendly forces: subparagraph will provide information detailing all superior, adjacent, attached, and supporting units. It provides information detailing the unit location and mission.

II. Mission: this will be your mission statement. This is your task from your superior. It is the foremost paragraph of your order. It is a clear and direct statement of what your unit must accomplish. This statement will contain your: Who, What, When, Where, and Why.

III. Execution: this paragraph will detail how you plan to accomplish your mission. It will have three pertinent components.

> A. Concept of Operations: this is your tactical plan from the beginning to end of your mission. It will detail how you envision the mission to play out.
> B. Tasks: this is your order to your Marines. You will task them

on what to accomplish. This will be their mission statement down the chain of command. This is where you will dictate to each subordinate element what it is exactly you want them to accomplish.

C. Coordinating Instructions: this subparagraph will detail how you want movements, formation, fire (artillery and close air support) plans and any tasks pertinent to the mission. It will include phase lines and checkpoints.

IV: Administration and Logistics: will detail elements to aid in the mission. It will provide information on the rations, ammunition, aid stations, and prisoner of war controls. Short form is the four B's.

    A. Beans
    B. Bullets
    C. Band aids
    D. Bad guys

V. Command and Signal: paragraph information on the command element and the communication (signal) plans.

A. Command: will identify the chain of command should you and or subordinates be incapable of execution. It will identify who next will assume the mission. It will provide information on the location of the commander and command element.

B. Signal: will identify the communications plan. To include radio frequencies, nets, pyrotechnics, enemy signals, call signs (aliases), and how to communicate with higher and adjacent elements.

SMEAC is a bit dry for civilian consumption so thank you for bearing through its rigid detail. However, know this, every Marine who gives and takes orders does so in the form of the OpOrd. It drives everything we do as a Corps.

Dissemination: A platoon (42 Marines) commander will receive his order from a company commander. The platoon commander will then give his order to the squad (13 Marines) leaders. The squad leaders will then give their orders to the Fire Team (four Marines) leaders, and the Fire Team leader will give an individual order to the three Marines composing that team. In the order you are describing to them the battlefield, what's going on, what's taking place, who is doing what, where it's happening and why. The most important part of the order is the Mission. It's the heart, the root, the soul and the very foundation of success for the Marine Corps is mission accomplishment.

The Mission statement gives you focus. It gives you singularity. It takes the complexity of the battlefield and focuses a small group to execute on one task and see it through to completion. Boiled down in its basic form, it is: "You, do this":

You, Marines, go do this one thing.

Do not worry about, X, Y, Z, etc.

Just go do this one thing and upon completion you are successful.

Get it done as rapidly and expeditiously as possible to ensure its accomplishment.

Not with haste or reckless regard for planning, but with thorough understanding and a bias for action.

"Take this one thing I'm telling you to do, go get those Marines over there and get this done." That's it.

Bottom line up front, Marines exist for mission accomplishment. The training, the fighting, the uniform, the ethos, this history, everything comes down to this. The planes, tanks, artillery, machine guns, firearms, munitions, bombs, and grenades are nothing but tools that aid the process. They are nothing without an order. Recited above, discipline is "instant and willing obedience to all orders." **The**

United States has at any time ~180–200K trained killers, who endured the longest sustained basic training, courses, and schools, prepositioned around the world, who are all awaiting an order. Once it's received, *instant and willing*, they rapidly execute without question.

Quite powerful really. America has a quarter of a million Marines, on embassies, naval vessels, bases, installations, and camps awaiting an order for "you go do this." Really easy to sleep well at night knowing the US can call upon this resource to get something done. Who's on the receiving end of that phone call, is a commander who has a flock of *dudes* that just spent the past year shooting shit.

There are other nuances to the specific nature of each task. A core component left out of the original **SMEAC** is *Commander's Intent*. A key piece added at the turn of the century which falls directly into the Mission (most important part) of the OpOrd.

Commander's Intent: this will describe in three components how you specifically want the mission to be accomplished. It will give your intent to your Marines.

1. Purpose: this will allow you to express the reason you're being tasked to complete this mission.
2. Exploitation: will highlight how you want to exploit an enemy weakness and their critical vulnerability.
3. End state: this will be the definition of mission accomplishment. It will highlight the conditions that satisfy the purpose and deem a mission complete.

A commanders' intention gives clarity to the order. In case anything cannot easily be understood or comprehended, it provides the commander a free area to state what he wants you to do. It also gives the Marines an insight into what a commander wants completed.

As an overview:

Kilo Company Commander (Captain Redding) will give an order to his four Platoon Commanders. The mission statement for Capt

Redding will be from the Battalion Commander (Lieutenant Colonel Turner). In his order, he will state his own mission, as a commander as received from LtCol Turner and then give an individual task to each Platoon commander. The task each Platoon commander receives will now be their mission statement. That Platoon commander will now give a task to each individual squad leader. The task received from the Platoon commander will be the mission statement of the squad leader. And so on and so forth.

After reciting each mission statement, the commander will state his attention. Example of a Platoon commander's OpOrd:

> "[Mission statement] *On order, as the main element, 2nd Platoon will destroy the enemy position at objective alpha in order to support the company assault on primary objective bravo".*
> "[Commander's intent] *My intention for this attack will be a swift and overpowering movement on objective alpha in order to link up with Kilo company and assault on primary objective bravo. Objective alpha is in open terrain with limited warfighting personnel."* Then go on to task the individual squad leaders.
> What are we really saying with our intention? *"Hey, go in there and get this done as fast as possible so we can join the main attack."*

Throughout TBS, IOC, and my time spent in the fleet and deployed, everything we would do would be based upon this order structure and process. Every order would be written and then spoken to the subsequent commander and Marines in the chain of command.

Take note of these very crucial steps: **write it down** and **speak it aloud**.

Every war, every battle, every engagement and armed conflict in Marine history was preceded by a commander who wrote something down and gave his verbal command to someone else.
Nothing can be more crucial for any hopes of success later in life than speaking your intention aloud to the world.

Infantry Officer Course: Class 2-06 (January–March 2006).

Class dedication: JP Blecksmith, KIA 11-11-04 Fallujah, Iraq. USNA c/o 2003.

> "He is best who is trained in the severest school." – IOC headboard

There's been a series of physical adversities I've had to endure, mostly short in nature. Having been on the high school wrestling team for three years, your typical match is 3 x 2 minute rounds, six minutes of combined pain. For a typical tournament, you'd endure two to five total matches if you kept advancing. Maximum: 30 minutes of high intensity full exhaustion for a complete one-day tournament, assuming you'd made it to the championship round. Following high school, I continued to wrestle at the Naval Academy prep school in Newport, Rhode Island, which was mostly Division III schools with no recruited athletes. Total: four years of combined wrestling experience.

Following acceptance into the Naval Academy, not being anywhere near talented nor tough enough to join or walk onto a top tier, Division 1 Wrestling program such as Annapolis, I decided to try boxing. I'd always been a fan of boxing growing up. Watching the greats (Holyfield, Tyson, Oscar, Tito Trinidad) with my father and family, this gave me the opportunity to try the sport in action. The weight classes were similar, so cutting weight seemed to be in line with previous parameters of my background.

We'd train a series of circuits between bags, calisthenics, jump rope (of course), pull-ups, stairs etc. Practice would be capped, and we'd turn to more training of either a run or a swim afterwards. This was the peak physical conditioning of my life. I'd further opt for conditioning by skipping the occasional dinner and pounding several glasses of water before lunch, to lessen the caloric intake. My "fighting" weight would be the 155lb weight class. As a 6' dark, lanky, Filipino dominant concoction of bones, I thought I'd be prepared for any go in the ring. I finished a combined two-and-a-half years of boxing, with a record of 0-2.

No matter how determined I was to cut weight, train, swim, run, physically endure, I'd get an intense amount of anxiety in the ring and could not control my breathing. I learned here the nervousness of being in the arena. Having wrestled for four years through high school and prep school, I thought fright of the arena would be forgone. At the least, I expected the experience of being on the wrestling mat would translate to preparation into boxing. My number one flaw: breathing.

Quoted so many times and never truer words, spoken by Mike Tyson, "Everyone has a plan until they're punched in the mouth." I cannot begin to praise the poignant effect of this statement. After years of training, cutting weight, circuits, etc. regardless of if I may have been in better shape than my opponent, *not saying I was*, it didn't matter. No amount of shape matters if you cannot control your breathing. Something I learned, not nearly soon enough. Keeping your cool, under pressure, while being pummeled in the face. Your plan, your training, your thoughts, all mean nothing, until you account for the series of blows coming to your body and face in full force. This can never be too discounted.

Midway through junior year, after skipping so many meals and not any success in the ring, I decided to forgo my boxing career and commit to enjoying my last two years at the academy by traveling with the Ultimate Frisbee Club (I was team president my senior year, zing!). These were great times indeed, and many fond memories on tournament fields up and down the North East. Clearly, no means in comparison to the lessons endured in the ring.

This brings me to January 2006, when following completion of the six-month mandatory course for young Marine Officers, *The Basic School (TBS)*, I would endure the hardest time period of my life at that time, **USMC Infantry Officer's Course (IOC)**. With little flair for advertisement or advocacy, the school headquarters in Quantico, VA, had a wooden headboard at the entrance with the following: "He is best who is trained in the severest school."

I can only describe this grueling 13-week course which combines sophisticated tactical training, classic maneuver warfare, and shear gut wrenching physical endurance as a **test of your willpower**. That's all it is. After four years at the Academy preparing to be an officer and six months of instruction as a Marine Corps Officer in The Basic School, IOC is the cherry on top. It is the last arena before being sent out to the fleet to lead Marines during a time of war. With sustained combat operations taking place in Iraq and Afghanistan, this would be the greatest test of mettle for any man and woman. Not seeking the fanfare of high attrition rates posted by various military schools and courses, IOC simply wanted to ensure you could be trusted to lead Marines in combat. The only way to do that would be through sheer perseverance, both mentally and physically.

Without the ability to share all its intricate details, I can only highlight that January in Virginia is rather cold. The first hurdle, before jumping into the arena is the Indoctrination Test. This was a full day, sixteen-hour endurance course where you're dropped off in the middle of the woods, in a dark, cold Virginia winter, where you have to navigate to checkpoints in the rain and complete armed physical tasks (nonstop) through late evening.

Thirteen weeks felt like a dream (nightmare if you will) of where you started, and somehow, eyes open, you kept pushing through the woods in Virginia, only to find yourself on the other side of a forest in March, upon the start of spring, with orders in your hand. You can recall every exercise, run, plunge, and maneuver with distinct detail; however; you'd rather just glance over the memories as a vivid recollection. Every fight you endured, every dip of tobacco, every order you gave and received, fully embedded into your brain core are nothing more than just faint memories.

A typical IOC class, 50–80 Marine Officers, over the course of 13 weeks will expend more munitions than an entire Marine Infantry

Battalion (~800 Marines) will utilize during a year of training. Aka, we shot shit. That's all we would do, train, fight, and shoot stuff all fucking day. "Attack this hill, go blow it up. March 10 miles over there, go blow up that hill. Run back six miles over there, go shoot that fort." For weeks on end, we'd navigate the woods of Quantico, in the field all week, full pack, humping[3] all hours of every day and shoot more shit.

Everywhere we went, we were running or full pack humping all gear and munitions en route to shoot something. Between live fire activities, we'd ground fight each other, box, train, eat, chew tobacco, then go somewhere else and do it again. It was modern day Spartan training for three months straight. In the words of (then Captain) Major Brian Chontosh[4] we were "dudes doing dude shit." Every activity would grow in size and scale over the course of those thirteen weeks. From small team, four-man, live fire (shooting shit) activities, to full-on platoon- and company-size engagement where we were inserted with Amphibious Assault Vehicles (AAV) or helo[5] inserted, the magnitude in size of force and munitions (willpower) we'd inflict grew. Those thirteen weeks were then capped off with a visit to the desert of 29 Palms, California (the largest military installation in the US) where we would run every range, encampment, and mock town and guess what, we would be shooting more fucking shit. Upon the final exercise, an evening raid lasting four to six hours on the hardest course in 29 Palms, I would be stationed on the machine gun hill with a team of gunners where we would provide overhead cover for the sustained attack. For a quarter of a day, throughout the middle of the night, our machine gun position would dump well over 10K–20K rounds that night. Barrels would start to glow fluorescent from the expenditure. Between changing ammo cans, multicolored tracer rounds zipping out, and red glowing barrels, we laid amongst a mountain of 7.62mm casings. It looked like a pile of gold, and we were scrooge swimming in machine gun riches at completion of that final exercise.

(I do not care to own a firearm now as a civilian, just because I don't think there's more stuff I need to shoot anymore. How much gunpowder does one really need to smell in their life?)

One winter evening I dislocated my arm during a midnight ground fight, full gear, in a bunker in some ambiguous range. Flailing on the ground in immense pain, unable to see anything as the fight took place in a total blackout room, three Captain instructors looked down upon me with night vision goggles like aliens operating on unknown specimen. Thankfully, Captain Mainz (now Lieutenant Colonel retired) as a former collegiate wrestler was equipped to heal my luxation as he'd witnessed detached limbs in his past, or at least I think he did. Popping it back into place instantly, I went on back to training with no recovery period. Having completed this grueling 13-week course, with a sustained injury along the way, was and will remain the hardest test I will endure in life.

Everyone thinks they're hard. They all think they had the toughest upbringing, the toughest parents, the hardest [insert bullshit here], the hardest coach/team, blah blah blah—and trust me, I was no different either. I thought I was actually a "tough" person as well. Years of sports, the academy, my upbringing, I thought I could handle most anything. I thought I endured the weather of difficult "training." I had not, up until that point. IOC kicked my ass, it broke me. Mentally, physically, structurally—I was broken down over those thirteen weeks. It was a bitch beyond proportions. Which is why it was designed; it did exactly it's job. The Marines Corps will break you down and then build you up so they can give you this new identity. IOC was the finishing completion of that transformation.

In summary, you graduate feeling like Superman!

Following IOC, I would go on to Basic Intelligence Officer Course (Dam Neck, Virginia), Scout Sniper Platoon Leaders Course (Quantico, Virginia), and receive orders to go on to my first Infantry Battalion: 3rd Battalion, 7th Marines (3/7). Our battalion motto, "The Cutting Edge". Our callsign, "Blade". What better logo could I have for the cover of my book that aptly describes my experiences, my first battalion, and the Marine Corps ethos than a **KA-BAR**[6]? Even more fitting for executing any *Recipe*, the mandatory requirement chiefly being a blade or knife.

I would first serve as a rifle platoon commander of 2nd Platoon with Kilo Company, 3/7, then transition to Assistant Intelligence Officer, then Intelligence Officer (S-2) over the next three years. Over those 36 months, we would deploy twice, both to Iraq (Ramadi and Al Qaim) in the Sunni-dominated area along the Euphrates, West of Baghdad. Including the time spent for the work-up[7] and time deployed, I would spend twenty-six of the next thirty-six months in the field, in the desert in Iraq or otherwise training in some capacity.

Iraq—"The motherfucking cradle of civilization"

During our second deployment to Al'Qaim, Iraq, I had the privilege of manning our turret gun on the lead HMMWV. Upon every patrol, mission, movement, and convoy I'd get on the mic and with a high-pitched, feverish yell "The motherfucking cradle of civilization boys." I found this call to be humorous, truthful, and grounding. One patrol, on a late afternoon (4–5pm) we finished, right outside the last checkpoint before you head into Syria. A "no go" zone for US and Iraqi forces, our dual convoy stopped at a Combat Outpost on this cliffside for a look over the border. Perched on those Iraqi bluffs several hundred feet overlooking the Euphrates River, the setting sun broke through the gray covered clouds and lit up the water with a million twitter sparkles throughout that densely cropped green valley. This was the fertile crescent. The birthplace of human civilization. The record of humanity started right here. With a cigarette in hand, I took off my flak jacket and Kevlar helmet, then forever etched this picture into memory.

We would spend those seven months of deployment on the border of Iraq and Syria, patrolling an open desert with our fellow Iraqi Army brethren. We would live, eat, drink, and join our Iraqi brothers, on their own base, for seven months of training and missions. Time spent mostly chasing cigarette and oil smugglers in the black market of Arab trade. Personally, this was a cultural evolution to spend with these Iraqi warriors. My translator, Mohammed, even got me a goat for my birthday. I nicknamed him RAMbo, because even as a scrawny and scroungy leaf eating mammal he had some sharp and pointed horns protruding past his ears. We ate him three months later at our final meal with the Iraqis before heading back home. Poor RAMbo.

I don't care much for detailing the deployments or daily life in Iraq further, another book for another day. I'll leave this up to an untold Marine who has a much better panache for detailing a combat deployment. However, I can and do want to share with you the immense honor and pride I still to this day have when I look back at our accomplishments during that time period. During our first deployment to Ramadi (the war-torn peak capital of the insurgency), our intelligence team drove and produced target packages that led to the capture, higher prosecution, and detainment of 34 High Value Individuals (HVI), aka insurgents. A platoon of men with ties and full dealings with then the Islamic State of Iraq (ISI), now the Al-Qaeda in Iraq (AQI) or the *Levant*, were taken off the streets and otherwise sent to higher detention facilities. In several cases, we were able to send three insurgents all the way to the Criminal Case Courts of Iraq (CCCI), for the highest level or prosecution due to their involvement with attacking and killing US service members. Several received the death penalty for the level of proof and intelligence work we were able to provide in their conviction. All those months, years, and hardship-endured training—this was the culmination of our combined efforts as a team: a few less assholes off the street. In the years following (2011–2013), as Al-Qaeda took back portions of Iraq and Syria, they would destroy towns, kill innocents and enslave women and children. I can only hope the work we did those several years prior to take a few of those dickheads from this earth helped save a man, woman, or child that had to endure the raping and pillaging after US forces left Iraq.

> [Side bar: Any/all politics aside, Iraq is a beautiful country with beautiful, kind, energetic and hardworking people that, like all of us, only want the best for their future generations. Over the past 100 years, British and US forces have been the cause for their depletion as a nation. Caught in the predicament of actually having an abundant natural resource, oil, they've been victim to a century-long bloodthirst of outside intruders. They were the first of civilization and humankind was built upon the fertile crescent. They were the Sumerians and Akkadians that built Mesopotamia. They were the Babylonians. They were the Parthian Empire. The origins of our ancestors and first history of homo sapiens forming civilizations came from this place. Human history started here with agriculture, reading, writing, language, communication, math, and astronomy. The origination of knowledge and learning started in this beautiful area and spread from the banks of the Euphrates to form the known world. And we fucked them!]

From graduating Annapolis in May of 2005, to returning home

from our second deployment in spring of 2009 I was "away." The coming to life transition I had when heading to NAPS in summer of 2000 and committing those next 10 years to a life of service were now at a conclusion. I had completed what I originally set in my mind some 15 years prior as a 7th grade youth holding that originally formulated this plan of attending the Academy and serving my country which manifested into reality.

My checkboxes in life were complete:

Graduate the Academy—check.

Become a Marine—check.

Serve overseas during a time of armed conflict—check.

I was now back to that original starting point of wondering what I would do next. With no plans at all, this would be my downfall.

---

1. The Continental Marines were formed in Tun Tavern, on November 10, 1775, by the decree of the Second Continental Congress of 1775. The declaration of independence, marking the birth of the United States was signed on July 4, 1776. Thus, the Marines were formed before the birth of the United States.
2. The Operation Order, loosely referred to as OpOrd for short, is the mission given to a unit commander for dissemination that takes into account the environment, enemy, mission, and time. It is issued in a five-paragraph format to communicate the tactical plan to a unit.
3. Hump: made known during the Vietnam war, is military jargon to refer to a forced march or hike over long distance with war fighting equipment to engage an enemy unit.
4. In 2003, during Operation Iraqi Freedom (OIF), Chontosh was ambushed in Baghdad. He aggressively assaulted an entrenched enemy position and was reported to have killed 20 enemy combatants. He was subsequently awarded the Navy Cross.
5. helo is a slang term for helicopter.
6. Ka-Bar is the United States Marine Corps combat knife. Pronounced K-bar, it was adopted during World War II and has become a synonymous symbol of the US Marines.
7. Work-up period: traditionally six months in length, this is the training period for Marines to progress and qualify on combat maneuvers and tactical exercises. It reinforces small unit tactics and prepares a battalion size element for deployment abroad. Whether on a Marine Expeditionary Unit (MEU) or forward deployed to a combat environment.

FIVE

THE DOWNFALL

After my second deployment, and after returning back to 29 Palms in spring of 2009, I was exhausted. I was ready to get out of the Marines and go figure out life in some other capacity. I was clueless, I had no idea what I wanted to do. Made worse, I had no idea, no plans at all how I would live life after returning home. Five years spent on the East Coast in a college dungeon, constantly on restriction in some form or another, then another four in the hardest training possible, followed by two deployments to Iraq with a hardened and decorated battalion, 3/7, I was once again ready to hang it up.

There was really nothing more I wanted to do.

The cause of great failure in life: not wanting anything.

I spent my childhood years thinking, praying, preparing to go on and spend those past 10 years in service. I did what I set out to do, what more did I need to do in life?

At the end of our second deployment to Al'Qaim, my then Military Transition Team Commander Captain Ayers (now Lieutenant Colonel Ayers) made mention that there was a lot more to the Marine Corps than just a battalion and deployments. I told him I would consider staying on if the possibility of going to a big/real city,

Los Angeles or New York, and not being stationed on any base were possible. To my unknowing, he mentioned recruiting duty as a possible option.

In summer of 2009, I took orders to Recruiting Station Los Angeles where I would serve as the **Officer Selection Officer** (OSO) on USC. This meant that I would be responsible for trying to recruit college students, in Los Angeles, to join the Marines. They would remain in college and spend summers at Officer Candidate School (OCS) and then, following graduation from their respective university, they would go on to accept a commission to serve as Marine Officers.

In what seemed like an amazing tour of duty, stationed at USC, in Los Angeles, away from a base—there's one particular detail they failed to leave out, you had a quota. Another way for stating you had a recruiting quota, you received an order for monthly, quarterly, and annual attainment. A commanding officer would issue legally binding and constitutional orders to go out and find as many men, women, minorities, law school students, ground and aviation contract college students on USC and surrounding campuses as possible. The order would be broken down further by year group. Example: *by order, your quota for attainment needs to fulfill: xx Hispanic college juniors, xx African American sophomores, xx female freshman, xx first- and second-year law students, and of those groups this many sophomores, freshman and juniors have to be aviation contract guaranteed.* Aviation, meaning they had to pass a flight physical and with the highest standards pass an Aviation Selection Test Battery (ASTB).[1]

One can only imagine how hard it would be to convince a USC (or otherwise college) freshman-sophomore-junior to forgo their summer activities and voluntarily sign up for Marine Officer Candidate School (OCS), the hardest in the nation. The difficulty grows harder when convincing a law school student to do the same as well, especially when adding they must pass the bar following OCS and then go on to TBS. I thought I knew a shit show when I saw one, but those next 36 months of recruiting would be a proverbial slap in the face, following the kick in the nuts I just went through of back-to-back deployments; really the icing on the cake. Made worse, Los Angeles is a dangerously fun place for a Marine who just spent the past 10 years *away*.

I would relink with my childhood best friend, Josh Pascua and with a new circle in tow, Paul Salazar and new amigo Juan Gutierrez, we would all head to downtown Los Angeles for living arrangements. Promoted to the rank of Captain in 2010, I went on to ensure I blew every paycheck I had from there forward. What better way to spoil a decade of hard work than a convertible BMW M3? Surrounded by friends, a downtown apartment and dope whip, I would say my downfall started right around here.

Atop the training, development, and knowledge benefits you receive from being deployed or in the field all the time, you're also away from society. You've secretly been gifted this opportunity to excel when you're away from the pressures of making bad decisions. More importantly, you as a person are limited to nothing and surrounded by nothing in a desert. Therefore, the choices of making bad decisions are nonexistent. You really can't fuck up being in the middle of nowhere. The choices of making bad decisions as a newly promoted single Marine in Downtown LA are the exact opposite, they are limitless. Arising from the wake of the financial crisis in 2008–2009, LA came alive in 2010. With the downtown area birthing a revitalization project and the mainstream adoption of house music, aka electronic dance music (EDM), the city was popping. (By the way, I still hate that term EDM. Not that I mind the music and more importantly the DJ's making it mainstream, I think the acronym sounds childish.)

Slowly at first, then suddenly!

A downfall is a lot like a snowball rolling downhill. It starts, you see it forming, you think you can contain it, and then before you realize, it's uncontrollable and unstoppable. From 2010 through 2012, this was my snowball effect: continuous and utter drinking. Nonstop, every weekend I got the chance. Who am I kidding? I was the same on the weekdays too. Bars, nightclubs, weekends in Vegas, Hollywood, and the exploration of every enclave in Los Angeles, it was a two-year blow-off top.[2] Everywhere I went, everything I would do, there was alcohol involved at some point. I don't know if it was even fun anymore or just something you would do because you always had this need to be out doing something, and alcohol is the best accompaniment for social engagement. Recruiting all week and the drinking all weekend, this was the routine. It was fun for instances here and there but definitely not sustainable.

That tour of duty would come to an end when I was pulled over for a Driving Under the Influence (DUI) in fall of 2011. Later charged with an "exhibition of speeding," this marked the end of my life as a Marine. Not that I was kicked out or forced to leave, but this was definitely the wakeup call that my heart just wasn't in this life of service anymore. In order to be a Marine, you have to be all in. You have to be committed, every day, every waking hour, you have to be about this life. This is the mindset it takes to make it as a Marine, completely and utterly "all in." You can't drop your guard, you can't question your future, you have to know exactly why you're in this game and give it, give everything. You have to be fully dedicated. You can make mistakes, everyone does. No one performs perfectly over the course of a career, but you can't fuck up. Making a mistake and fucking up are distinguishable differences, and in the eyes of the Marine Corps, a DUI, not even a conviction, just being charged with one, made me a fuck up. In the words of my IOC lead and instructor, Captain Lappe (now Lieutenant Colonel Lappe) who told us on a winter day over a fireside discussion in the hills of Quantico "Once it's not about the Marines anymore, just get out. Do us all a favor and get out." No truer words can resonate.

I submitted my resignation papers a month or so later and would finish out my time in a depressive state of letdown. My commander at the time, Major William 'Bunge' Cook (now Colonel Cook) in his disappointment (and probably disgust for my action) and in an effort to provide counsel as he could see I was in need of guidance offered me this, "Jake, do you have a mentor in life?" Not understanding the full effect of the question, I responded with my father. He immediately shook his head and said I know your dad isn't your mentor. Not as a slight to my dad, just that he knew I did not indeed have a mentor. Someone to talk about life with. Someone to provide a non-biased, nonjudgmental opinion on the course of your life. I did not have a mentor. I didn't know we needed one to navigate life. Now I know. Everyone needs someone in life. I would later find mentors in both my managers and private coaching. *Thank you Bunge!*

In order to get my DUI reduced to an exhibition of speeding citation, I had to accept a sentence of community service, two weeks, give or take I believe. In my last few weeks in the Marines, I didn't have the option of taking two weeks off. Truthfully, I just didn't feel like taking my weekends off to go work on the side of the Los Angeles highway system in an orange jumpsuit. In our combined mutual shock, the LA prosecuting attorney said "Sure, if you don't want community service, I can send you to county[3] for the weekend." I didn't realize he was joking at the time with his offer, nor did he realize I was excited for the switch. He gave me this perplexed look as if to say, *are you sure you want this?* To his amazement, I responded with an equally delighted face of *yes, this I'll definitely take this offer*. What he didn't realize and what many I tell this story seem to forget—for me, the decision was simple, go spend three days in a concrete confinement or spend 14 days slaving outside? Up to this point, I'd lived in a concrete dormitory for four years, spent several months on restriction at NAPS, and just wrapped up two back-to-back deployments in Iraq. I'd weathered IOC, after a dislocated limb. Three days in an air-conditioned cell with guaranteed free food was like a weekend at Cliffside.[4]

For anyone curious what life is like inside the Los Angeles County Men's Jail, the *Twin Towers*, correctional facility located on the north end of Downtown Los Angeles off of Vignes street, surprisingly not half bad. I checked in on a Thursday (or was it Friday morning?) and much to the prosecution's surprise, he asked what I was doing there. "Checking in for my sentence" I retorted. In his years of public service, I suppose the "typical" visitors arrive through other means. You go to a holding facility and then are bused to a check-in point. You take a shower and then throw on matching outfits, dark blue pajamas like pullovers with thick sock booties and black slip-on ninja shoes. Everyone is in there for drugs. They're all just kids, getting caught doing stupid shit, hyped up on drugs. Our jail system is a weekend detention facility for the cracked-out minorities of Los Angeles. Amongst the 50-odd inhabitants of my check in, I think there was one white kid (maybe half-white even) who was brought in for joy riding in a stolen car, probably on drugs. By drugs, it's all methamphetamine, aka speed. All of them, hopped up on meth/crank/ice, and they're all kids. Late teens, early twenties, skinny, strung out lost children, all minorities, running around the streets of South and East Los Angeles. Speed has an unknown and terrible nickname on the street, it's called "shit." No, literally, the nickname is actually "shit". "You have any shit ... we were coming down off shit last night ... let's get some shit," that's the actual nickname.

 What's even worse, if you look at the chemical makeup of the most commonly used drug to treat ADHD (*Adderall, Desoxyn*) it's actually the same exact shit. Chemically, Adderall is a mixture of four amphetamine salts.[5] So, the same exact narcotic we're arresting teens and youth minorities for all over Los Angeles and probably every major metropolitan area in the US is actually being legally prescribed by major pharmaceutical companies. Adderall was the 24th most commonly prescribed medication in the United States, with more than 25 million prescriptions.[6] Probably not a surprising nor shocking fact that 8% of the US population has a prescription for the exact same drug incarcerating our nation's youth, mostly consisting of minority inner city homes. Clearly drugs and narcotics are not the problem if we're prescribing the same chemical to 8% of all US households, but incarcerations for controlled substances are all predominantly composed of minorities. Way to go 'Murica!

I left the Marines on September 30, 2012. Just several weeks before my 30th birthday. No going away, no celebration, no thank you, no good-bye. I was given a stacked file of medical records and military discharge papers, then walked out of the building. Thankfully, I had several months of leave (vacation/PTO) saved up, so I received a nice $10K check that sunny afternoon. It promptly went directly into paying off the credit card bills I had racked up over the past several years. So here I was, 30 years old, combat veteran, former Marine Officer, with nothing more than the clothes on my back that I joined the service with 13 years prior as a dumb 17-year-old high school grad. I suppose the memories are a noteworthy accumulation, however they don't really buy you a beer at the bar.

The Breakdown

[7]Upon my departure from the Marines in the fall of 2012, I was on a mission to consume as many drugs and drink as much alcohol as possible. My DUI and subsequent incarceration was just a steppingstone into a much grander splash of degeneration. I was on a mission of self-hate, pure and simple.

> [Sidebar: Anyone that destroys their body through any gluttonous means of overconsumption, whether it be drugs, alcohol, porn, narcotics, sugar, etc.—they hate themselves. They just don't know it. So, if you're reading this, now you're aware.]

There's a societal negative connotation that incarceration of any form is bad. Taken to a worse degree, any form of reprimand is bad. This creates a fictitious divide in the mind of those who've never actually made a mistake in life in thinking they're "good." When, in fact, they're just in a state of being "not in trouble." My brief blip in the county abode revealed that the halls were not lined with "bad" kids, just those with little concern for a societal connotation. Myself included.

This connotation or way of thinking also forms the basis for mediocrity in the future. Parents of every juvenile being raised now postulate that not being in trouble is "good." Therefore, not failing is also good. When, in fact, failure is the ultimate tool for doing anything great. Failure is the ultimate teacher of success.

I don't particularly know why, after leaving home at 17 and spending the next 13 years of life in education and service, I probably felt some sort of entitlement to this punishment I was about to pursue. Two deployments and seven years leading Marines in the fiercest military branch in the world during a time of conflict, I was now ready for nothingness. No responsibility, no planned job or career, NO PURPOSE. I was ready to be nothing to society, and really if I am honest, nothing to myself. I was ready to give up. My therapy would be destruction, not of the world but of self.

In hindsight some years later, this is utterly ridiculous to think you're entitled to fucking up your life. No one is entitled to hate, whether internal or hatred for the world around you. It's a choice. A lazy choice for those who have nothing else to be happy or excited about. They have nothing to chase. Nothing to love or pursue. Since they have nothing, they are nothing. Therefore, they hate.

For anyone that's ever wondered what "full tilt"[8] looks like, it's this exact description in live form: the inability to make any correct decision.

My week would typically go something like this:

Wake up, groggy, semi-melancholy, take a walk, then take an Adderall for awareness followed by another one for extra "umph," meander, try to do something productive, get lunch (more than likely at Panda Express or a burrito), take some more Adderall, probably try to go to the gym or a run, have a sense of accomplishment that the previous night's alcohol was out of my system, then smoke some weed by late afternoon either from the bong, or a personal favorite was the grape wrapped XXL papers, start drinking, and then the day would really start.

If it was a Monday, boring, nothing to do other than stay home and play video games while forcing as much weed into the lungs as possible. Tuesday thankfully was "Taco Tuesday!" so any bar was a great place for cheap food served with Coronas 'n Margaritas. By Wednesday, it was hump day, thus entitled to something a little livelier as the week is half over and you've made quite the accomplishment in getting this far. Then came Thursday, which basically meant it was pre-Friday, and the perfect time to start actually partying at a bar or now a club. People were a lot more inclined to go out Thursday nights, so this normally gave you company to push the degenerate level further. By Friday night, it's time to unleash full retard. This is where the hard drugs come into play (ecstasy, cocaine, and the sorts, really anything you can get your hands on) and you're trying as methodically as possible to combine all of them together for a miraculous concoction that doesn't black you out but does give you pure euphoric elevation.

Rolling into Saturday, you're at full climax. The day drinking starts, and well… so does every other drug mentioned. You're getting high at breakfast, at lunch, and continuously throughout the day. The Adderall has now been crushed and snorted as a means of injection, and by dinner time of course the night just gets started and you're anywhere but at home.

My preferred location was a rave house named Avalon, where not only did I get to become familiar with their doorman, but also their main drug dealer. This place wouldn't close until 5am, so nights were long. Sunday was a hazy awakening, where your mind can not stop ringing and the beats from yesterday's night are still pumping full blast in your head. The best part about Saturday nights debauchery, is the music stays with you for a full 24 hours later on repeat, nonstop. The perfect concoction on a Sunday afternoon to wave off the damage from last night is a malt liquor of both tasty flavors and nasty ingredients, the "Four Loko." This blend of alcohol and caffeine is the nitroglycerin of the intoxicant world. It should be banned. (I actually think it was at some point in time after a fraternity killed several pledges from mass consumption.) However, lethal its combination may be, it's powers to neutralize the degenerative powers of the Friday/Saturday combo mentioned above is wonderful. In fact, if you drink enough of these (probably around three tall cans), you hit another state of euphoric degeneration I've aptly nicknamed being "Four Loko'd"™ (dibs on trademark). The Sunday evening "Four Loko'dness" starts to wear off as you switch back to the multiple bong hits and video games, giving you a nice sleep into Monday, where the cycle starts afresh. The weed has now gone from a "drug" to get high to a medicine to get you stable.

Intermission

For all of us who were once lost, in pain, angry, defeated, disappointed, confused, and utterly broken, this book is for you. This book is for the days we say *no mas*.[9]

This book is for the masses of lifeless souls wandering without direction. Lostness and confusion, possibly the worst states of being.

This is for the families and broken hearted, left in the wake of those same lost souls.

This is for those looking for a greater understanding of the meaning of forgotten and abandonment.

At least with failure, we can learn and pick ourselves up again. With not trying, you're in the dark and don't even know it. Trying and failing, this is okay. Giving up is simply unacceptable. There is no sweet without the bitter and for anyone who's never tasted *the sweet*, I write these words as a testament of change. We all go through the struggle at some point or another in life. I don't care about your money, your wealth, your background, your religious or spiritual beliefs, or your accomplishments. In fact, it's oftentimes people with the most who live through the struggle harder because they're continuously disappointed with trying to overachieve. This is by no means a knock to the less fortunate who everyday have to hustle to pay bills. No, this is a nod to the communal lost angels who've hit rock bottom.

You will undoubtedly one day be in the struggle. It is the truest form of hurt. I challenge anyone who is actually living their life to say they never have been hurt. If so, kudos to your ability to lie to yourself.

Pity

Thinking that by any means your background, your upbringing, your childhood were unfortunate and taking pity on yourself is nothing more than giving up. There's one thing after everything I've seen over the years, people care as little as they need to. Your ability to have any pity on yourself, for anything, is lost on the world. No matter how hard your life was before this, I can attest, if you're alive, you have the ability to push for more.

Pity is a powerful weapon, spoiling many of the great minds of our youth and future. Should you succumb to its addiction, it will give you exactly what you want: an excuse. It will always be there. Bearing its fruit to fill your desire. Your desire to give up, to not even try. Think about that, pity will stop you from NOT EVEN TRYING. Not testing yourself. Do not give into this powerful wonder drug of despair.

That pity you take on yourself is the worst drug in existence. Once you get a taste, it's an incurable addiction. It will prey on you at all times of the day and night. It will convince your subconscious to turn on you if allowed. Alcohol, sugar, narcotics, tobacco—fail in comparison.

There is one hope for you.

It is an addiction to yourself. A daily addiction to your habits, your wants, your power, your why. This is the cure. To your laziness, ineptness, and fear. It's an addiction to yourself. The remedy is reading your *Recipe* daily. It will free you. I offer this to you, as a lonely

Marine who's always questioned whether or not I'll pull through an adversity.

It is yours now.

Do not deny nor delay its power.

The closest brother to pity is entitlement, thinking the world owes you something. Thinking that for whatever reason what you did before this exact moment is some pre thought that you're guaranteed something in the future. I don't care what you've done, what you've accomplished, how many badges, awards, degrees, medals, accomplishments you claim to your possession. Nor does the world at large. The only determinant of your future success is that you keep pushing for more. Keep finding and seeking out adversity. I applaud you for your accumulation of accomplishments, and your wall loves the frames, but the world has no notion of who you are and what you've done unless you are out there wanting more, every, single, day.

In summation: No one fucking cares about what you did before. What you went through nor really what you "intend" to do. The world owes you this: a fuck you.

Only you can push yourself for more.

Wake up and take it every day.

No one is waiting, it's up to you.

Go out there and fight for your unfair share.

I wish you luck!

Godspeed.

---

1. MARADMIN 064/11: for those requesting to commission with an aviation military occupational specialty, a minimum score on the aviation selection test battery (ASTB) is required.
2. Blow-off top is a pattern found in stocks that have gone through a hyperbolic move (increase) upwards. It is rapidly followed by a significant downward drop in price action and exhaustion of buyers and holders.
3. *"County" is a* slang term to refer to your local county or municipal jail.
4. Cliffside Malibu is a well-known rehabilitation facility in Malibu, CA, internationally recognized for its top-notch, personalized care and proven treatment protocol. It's rehab for rich people.

5. If you look at the chemical makeup of Adderall, it contains a mixture of amphetamine salts. These same amphetamine salts can also be found in methamphetamine.
6. Provided by the ClinCalc DrugStats Database.
7. Breakdown: A failure of a relationship or system
8. Tilt is originally a poker term used to describe the state of a player who's at wits end and unable to execute their strategy accordingly. Full tilt has been widely spread to describe any sort of gambler who's in a place of deep losses and incapable of stopping.
9. "no mas": Spanish for "no more." Made famous in the second of three bouts between Roberto Duran vs Sugar Ray Leonard. Duran, at the end of the 8th round, turned to the referee and said "no mas." I quit.

SIX

THE WAKEUP CALL

In October 2012, Kendric Lamar released the album *Good Kid, M.A.A.D City*. It was an instant success and repropelled West Coast rap back to the top. It woke up Los Angeles, reaffirmed the greatness of Dr. Dre and established Kendric as a heavyweight. 'The Recipe' was a lead single on the album, in itself enough to cement Kendric's supernatural talent. The lyrics, a homage to what defines Southern California: *women, weed, & weather*. It would serve as the anthem for my post Marine life.

Summer of 2013, I really thought this was it at the time, this was all you needed: Women, weed, and weather. This was my *Recipe* at that very moment. *The Recipe* I needed to define how I'd break into my thirties. After four years at the Naval Academy and seven to eight years in the Marine Corps, I was fucking exhausted. I was spent and depleted of energy. That yearlong bender of partying seemed like my personal welcome home party after 13 years of being *away*. I couldn't think of a much better way to really forge the next chapter of my life, other than not forge one at all. So, why not adopt the lyrics of Kendric Lamar, "women, weed, and weather," and use them as my sound board for living?

Riding with my two high school best friends, Josh and Eddy, through the South Redondo Beach Esplanade, mid-afternoon, passing a J[1] back and forth between us—this was it, I needed nothing else to suit me in this very moment. No long-term plan, no goal, just the sun's warmth as we *no-hands* on the grip, rode our bikes from the coastal view flat, several blocks were all that separated us from the two-bedroom joint living space and the Italian Ice, sugar water latent chain Rita's franchise venture we decided to open.

Could you think of a better way you'd want to define a chapter of your life? We were quite literally selling ice cream on the beach (sure, Italian Ice if you want to be specific), without a care in the world and no plans to alter my current state of being. The vivid description, probably better suited for the summer of a teen ready to head off to college, was all I needed at that moment. Looking back, I pleasantly smirk and shake my head in humorous disbelief of the same view you're probably thinking: Three thirty-year-old latent men, traffic jamming the sun-drenched Redondo strip, waking and baking their way to a seasonal dessert establishment.

I've always been a fan of Dr. Dre. When he released *the Chronic* in the 90s, it was the first CD I ever purchased and my entry from adolescent to pre-pubescent teens. He (Dre) went on to discover other talented artists in the Los Angeles region, from Ice Cube to Snoop Dog. When he started working with Kendric Lamar in 2010, it's like the glory days of Rap from growing up in Pomona, California in the 80s–90s were back in full motion again. His production of symphonic beats and overleveraged use of bass are still to this day a masterpiece. Combined with Kendric's lyrics and vocal talents, the duo combination is the testament to California lifestyle.

Women: After three years of having navigated the *break-up-to-make-up* cycle I'm sure many couples are familiar with, Carol (my then girlfriend of three years) and I were in a good spot. As good as any, to be assured we were a real couple. She fit my view of the ideal mate. Tall, Asian, large breasts, compassionate, liked to party. She'd be there to make sure I always had enough fun, but never too much. She was my rock. She'd been there for the best and worst that I had to give life. The drinking, the debauchery, my DUI, my weekend county jail incarceration, she was there. Steadfast to ensure I didn't go too far down the rabbit hole, I'm sure she was scathed, but not broken and resolute we came out together as a stronger couple. See more about your rock later.

Weed: After leaving home at 17 to start my military life and two combat deployments to Iraq in 2007 and 2008–2009, I thought myself well deserved to spend every waking hour after my separation from the Marines in late 2012 to consume as much as possible of this wonderful herb.

Weather: The California climate really is a testament to perfection. With all-year-round sun and single digit rainy days throughout, I thought that growing up with a hoodie as a single piece of winter clothing was typical for the average American. Between winters in the northeast of Rhode Island and Annapolis, a hurricane in 2004 and then the next seven years spent training in wooded rainy terrain of Quantico, two deployments and countless exercises, I was never going to live outside California again.

The South Redondo Esplanade is a beautiful stretch of coastline, hidden well within the South Redondo Beach strip right before the Palos Verdes cove. When I saw it for the first time, for me, it was reminiscent of the Amalfi Coast/Lake Como in Italy. Not that I've ever been to either area, but really the symbolic view that this was it. If you've found yourself here, there was nowhere else to go.

In what would be the best unknown blessing to happen in my life, Carol got pregnant in summer of 2013, and I would soon be a father. This would be the wakeup call I would need to finally get back on track with life. I was ready for this. I was ready to stop running, stop destroying, ready to grow up, ready to commit, ready to start the next journey of my life. The future would be very unknown from here on out. The chapter in life from when I was 12 years old through 30 would now be closed. An 18-year wild run filled with ups, downs, and everything in between would usher its way to the next door in life. A life of service, a life of education, and partying and pushing the limits would be at an end. My time in the Marines would be at an end and now I would need to navigate the civilian world broke, hopeful, and a family in tow.

Tactical Maneuver

[2] Life is a series of making decisions and changes, they come in all forms. We all make bad decisions, some worse than others. Sometimes we keep making bad decisions until the world around us looks like a pile of shit and we have no idea which way is up or out. This location and time in life was the hole I would have to dig myself out of. It was peak summer in 2013, I'd gotten out of the Marines in 2012, did a weekend in county, had to wrap up the legal and attorney fees, then started a business with my pothead friend (completely underwater and underfunded), was maxed to the tit on every credit card to keep things afloat, and now would be having a child in eight months. A predicament indeed for most but, I was hopeful. I was a Marine, and once a Marine, always a Marine.

Up until this point in life, by now I'd figured out how to navigate most any difficult situation. I'd pushed, I'd trained, I'd traveled, I'd fought, I'd been injured and wary, I'd been incarcerated and deployed, I'd been in trouble and restricted more times than I could count. As long as you have a mentally positive outlook on the future, you can figure anything out. Really, all I needed to do now was get out of this hole and get back on track in life. The motivation of having a child is like none other. It takes women (God bless them) nine months (270 days) to grow a human being in their body. What also takes place during this beautiful, blessed time of growth is the realization it takes a man to come to terms with being a father. It's a 270-day wakeup call of 'get your shit together'.

So, get my shit together I had to do.

There's no harder small business in the US than the restaurant industry. Selling a seasonal product (like ice cream/dessert) meant you had peak and trough months, aka not steady income, which is made worse when you have no idea what you're doing, you're always behind. Josh and I opened Rita's in March of 2013; by that summer it was evident neither of us were cut out to be in charge. We literally ran that store into the ground. With the options of trying to raise a family on 50% of the net profits of a seasonal business and essentially anything else, I chose the latter. Thankfully, there's a huge recruiting industry for former Military Officers, particularly academy grads that wanted to get into sales. Armed with the phone numbers from several of the larger firms in the US, I started dialing to find the next hiring conference in California. I had very simple requirements, I wanted to be in sales, and I needed to stay in California.

My first conference was a success, I found two companies with positions opening up that fall and with my immediate timeline to start, they were also eager for a semi-young motivator to join their ranks. In October of 2013, after several rounds of interviews, in person flights, negotiating, I was able to land a "Field Sales Engineer" role with Amphenol Corporation in San Jose. Carol and I would move up north that same month and with a full U-Haul trailer and eight-month pregnant wife, the next chapter in life was about to start. The change to being a corporate man, a family man, a "still figuring it the fuck out" man would commence, and I'd find myself in a new area, with a new family and new chase in life.

Life in the Bay Area was a much-needed cooling off period that was perfect for a new father. Jaden Zeddidiah Cosme (*Zedd,*[3] yes named after the DJ) was born on November 5, 2013. Carol and I, in a new location in life, would explore, grow as a couple, get married, raise Jaden and transition to this parenting gig of our thirties.

Work would be a hustle and planning my corporate career was also fun. I found out there's no limit to what you want to do, and the only requirement was hard work. While in the Bay Area I was exposed to the tech world in full force. Working for Amphenol got me exposure to: Cisco, Google, Facebook, Yahoo, and Twitter. I was learning a new trade and developing a work ethic required for progressing in my career. Met with some initial (very) big victories of closing deals with Cisco early in my time, I felt as though the shit hole might finally have some light at the end.

The nice part about the corporate world, you always had objectives, it was very much like recruiting in the Marines and the missions you received when deployed. Every objective was just another form of a mission statement. If you wrote your mission (objective) down, as trained early on as a Marine, and kept it at your forefront daily, it served as a great tool for hitting targets. (Why doesn't everyone think of this?) The cold calling, the email outreach, the pushing, were all very similar tools we used in USMC recruiting as well. A few months later, we closed the Google account. This would go on to be a massively huge deal that I unfortunately would not stay around to reap the benefits from. Then a big Yahoo datacenter deal and positioning several opportunities at Facebook. I was building relationships at each of the companies and the Bay Area in general started to feel like home. Building my career, my family, and my professional resume was the start of my next chapter in life.

This field would be the new proving grounds in life for me. Much like navigating the backwoods of Quantico for months on end, the corporate hustle would be my new schtick. It was fun, it was rewarding, and I actually enjoyed those new experiences I would add under the belt. With victories along the way, this also started to feel like a new calling. However, I was met with another breakdown in life. The death of my father came in August of 2015 after a short-fought battle with cancer.

This left me very distraught and broken. The impacts would take some time to heal. Feeling the need to move back to Southern California, we would leave the Bay Area and the tech capital of the world to chase another role in the media landscape. I would go on to work at Verizon Media and learn an entirely new technology and career field in "Solutions Engineering," then grow through the ranks and change companies a time or two before eventually landing at a new and challenging startup. I'd get the chance to work with Hulu,

Roku, Fox, NFL, the Super Bowl, and grow deeper into my technical career. Challenges and accolades would accompany, the development would continue, and that lostness in life I'd endured since a child eventually grew to a close. I made the transition from the military, and now the corporate chase would be host to new yet unseemly less adventurous experiences. Life had eventually caught up with me or vice versa.

Proving

My wife is my rock in life, my anchor. Looking back before that, it was my father. His early death at the age of sixty left an open wound for me. I filled it, with alcohol mostly, as best I could, but his departure was traumatizing. Having a rock in life is not a main ingredient for *The Recipe*, but it is a perfect place for you to get started if you're properly lacking creativity, purpose, and desire. Much like Carol and Jaden lifted me out of the depths of self-destruction as I was lost right after the Marines, my dad was the rock of inspiration for me to go to the Academy and pursue a life of service.

If you don't have something you're chasing or pursuing, no worries, this is okay. It's often hard for people, with abuse, with neglect, with wander, to truly manifest their desire. We're a culture and economy of withdrawal syndrome. We're often raised, told, and most importantly preached that denial of the self is the best path in life. Humility and hubris are expansions of denying the self even further. There is a certain extent of discipline and commitment needed to formulate your true want in life, but it's often embedded in roundabout ways of making you work for something or someone. Concepts like hard work and service, more often than not, are used for anything but your true self. Your rock will relieve this undue burden, this pain of decades long traumatic syndrome. Your rock will release your ideas and serve as the foundation to expand themselves. And what is it?

It's the immutable formulation of proving something.
This is your rock.

This serves as the key to unlocking and opening up your purpose which will lead to your one WANT in life.

I want to reiterate it again, because this is a key theme as we get into building each ingredient of *The Recipe*. The underlying power that can make any person successful, regardless of background or upbringing, is the underlying want to PROVE SOMETHING. Prove something to your family/friends, to prove others wrong (very powerful), and then eventually prove something to yourself. Proving, combined with your subconscious is more powerful than any other asset in life.

Think about it, think of the times and people which recognize true success. The indisputable masters of the market. Their rock was a well embedded desire to prove others wrong. Was it done for themselves? For family? For some agnostic concept? IT DOESN'T MATTER. The ability to deepen desire for nothing but the sheer possibility of proof is enough. Now, look at yourself, your life, all of your accomplishments. Even the most talented and accomplished of actors continue to push, continue to conquer, and continue to succeed. Why? There's no quenching this thirst. It's forever. It's undying and when uncovered is your greatest arsenal for success. Think of the continued athletes who covet fame around the world (Kobe Bryant, Cristiano Ronaldo), think of their continued hard workday in and out that redefines: The act of being relentless.

How could anyone with such accumulated wealth and success continue to push their body and more importantly their mind to exhaustion after such feats of accomplishment? The need to prove more. It's that simple. It's the continued proof of life.

However, this proof, despite its ability to push and overcome does have its drawbacks. When not treated and nourished properly, it will manifest to the exact opposite of its intention. This is seen in such instances of greed, envy, piety (thinking you're a god). Which, over time, eventually leads back to the origin from which you started: neglect and abuse. Having a desire to prove something and not doing anything about it or taking action will surely fuck you up.

Think of the many times we've seen the meteoric rise and eventually fall of so many talented athletes and businessmen alike. As I stole his quote earlier in my story, "Everyone has a plan until they're punched in the mouth," Mike Tyson comes to mind when I think of this manifestation of proving to others, only to eventually be overcome and resort back to his primordial self. Again, back to his ways of abuse and neglecting, after losing the need to prove. Not enough words can go into the countless tales of broken-down women and men, who've succumbed to these same fates all over America.

For you, think about the many times someone has in your mind wronged you. The times you were broken up with by a significant other. The times you cried. The times you backed down from a fight. Ultimately, the times you were filled with fear. The times you were hit, spanked, denied as a child from your unruly parental figures. Denied something, anything. Denial itself is the underlying foundation. Entry to a club, a restaurant, a party. Taunted, bullied, and otherwise mocked in school, online, in your place of work. The instance, no matter how insignificant nor small nor inconsequential in life, is where you can draw upon an untold power lying deep within you. To the person who denied you: family, friend, or stranger, you can be thankful and happy they caused this adversity. This affliction you had to undergo of being denied at some point in life is a spark of wanting to prove something. For without it, there'd be nowhere else to draw upon this power. Even as I write, I need not give instances nor examples because you can feel the power of reminiscing flowing through you in this very instance. You can feel the many times, places, and emotions that this power emanates. It is stronger than perhaps your greatest achievements, if you were fortunate to have any in life up until this moment. It may even make you sad, melancholy and remorse for such an instance to occur, but you need this time right now to remind you, for there is no greater source for us to start the *Recipe*.

I ask you, think and think hard of these times in life you've been denied. Think of the emotions in that very instance you were presented with conflict. Let them flow and emit, then combine these small, seemingly unrelated events that have occurred throughout your life and bring them to the forefront of your mind to help you achieve and unlock their power. No need to share them nor write them down, the constant thought of harm done to yourself would only embolden the subconscious and mind to pain. We're not here for that. We're here for relief and success!

I wrote this to myself in 2018 before the birth of my second child, Maximilian Axwell[4] Cosme, after a brief dip in life.

```
From: jcosme@akamai.com
To: jakexcosme@gmail.com
Subject: Get your fucking shit together
Date: February 17, 2018 - 8:50pm

Get your fucking life together. You're on
tilt. You're a fucking druggie loser who's
ruining his family. And taking it out on
Carol. Get your fucking life together now!
But you can get it back. Be a man and step
the fuck up. Stop day trading you
degenerate. Stop drinking and doing drugs.
Start a strict workout routine ASAP!!!!!!!!
Stop blaming your wife. Quit spending and
save you fucking moron. Get it the fuck
together and you can pull yourself out of
this.
Pay off your credit card
Pay off your car
Max out every IRA for Carol and Jaden. Buy
```

```
stocks only!!!!!!! You get no control or
access.
Max out your IRA. Take away options.
Stop Trading!!!!!! No more options.
Quit spending! Immediately.
Stop all the bleeding.
Get it together!!!
No drugs!!!!
Less drinking. Start working out!!!
This is your goal!!!

From: jakexcosme@gmail.com
To: jcosme@akamai.com
Subject: re: Get your fucking shit together
Date: February 17, 2018 - 9:29pm
```

Write a book after this!

At the time of writing, I had just blown up my investment account. I had nuked my finances by making risky and volatile trades on equity options. That evening, sitting in the wallow of my own self-pity in our apartment, I had once again hit bottom. Like my 2013 breakdown of despair, I was once again in need of a wakeup call. Even harder this time around, I thought I was above making devastating bad decisions. I thought I had learned from past mistakes and the experiences would keep me from poor judgment calls in the future. No one is above making stupid choices in life. In just five years of passing from my departure of service, I was once again starting from the bottom.

With my father gone, my life of service complete, I now had to prove something to my family. To be the best and better man. I needed another wakeup call in life. This email was my reset to a life of living with virtue and values.

We all make mistakes, sometimes you need a swift kick in the ass to get you back on track in life. If that kick in the ass has to come from yourself, so be it.

The birth of my second son would make me push even harder in life now. From that day forward it was time to really get my shit together and start working on rebuilding. The resiliency it took to go through another wakeup moment in life was a testament to perseverance. This time consciously knowing I was prone to making constant mistakes, I knew I needed something to guide me. This was the very start of when *The Recipe* was formulated.

Everyone talks about hard work and grit when they're at the top. What about those at the bottom?

Where's the motivation for the lost souls stuck in the grind, stuck in the pits, looking for an exit?

The steadfastness, perseverance and resiliency it takes to pull yourself through the bottom, let alone multiple, tastes a bit different. For anyone looking to prove something, for anyone that wants more, that's not content with life, that needs a cheat sheet for success, here you go.

For anyone and everyone that's been in my position above, for everyone that's lost their money, suffered from depression, anxiety, alcoholism, [insert issue] _____* ism, been through pain and needs a way out, here are the ingredients to *The Recipe*.

---

1. J - short form slang for a joint of marijuana.
2. Tactical Maneuver is a theory developed in modern maneuver warfare where you make a calculated and abrupt movement during combat operations in order to gain an advantage over the enemy.
3. Anton Zaslavski, is a European DJ known as "Zedd." He's popularly known for electronic dance music (EDM) production.
4. Axel Hedfors is a Swedish DJ known as Axwell. He is one of three members of the group, Swedish House Mafia.

THE RECIPE

At the end of each of these "Ingredients" I have included two to three pages for you to write your own reflections so you can begin this process straightaway.

Your methodology is your own, and your future success is for you to own!

Now move it!

1. Your Purpose
2. Your Want
3. Your Intention
4. Your Habits
5. Your Affirmations
6. Your Strengths

INGREDIENT I – YOUR PURPOSE

"Singleness of purpose is one of the chief essentials for success in life, no matter what may be one's aim." – John D. Rockefeller

Situation: will contain information detailing the specifics and overall status of friendly and enemy forces.

YOUR PURPOSE IS YOUR SITUATION FROM THE OP ORDER

Your purpose is your WHY in life.

Why are you doing anything in life?

Like the situation tells the Marines about the good and the bad surrounding them, your why is a statement combined from your best and worst times of life. It gives premise to what is going on in your life and how you got there. Your purpose is based upon the stories of your past. It is your origin story from life's most impactful moments. These are very specific, meaningful moments that matter in your life's history. They may not necessarily be monumental and may possibly be seemingly innocuous. They are the greatest stories that involve other people. You can't find your why on your own, your stories will be filled with people that have made an impactful change in your life.

I came across the power of purpose at Akamai Technologies. After one-and-a-half years, I applied and was accepted to a Next Generation Leaders (NGL) program. I was pleased and excited to have the company acknowledge my contributions and offer a spot in this program with 30–40 various Account Executive and Technology Sales Leaders. The course was roughly 12 months, as an extracurricular design to expose a wave of Akamai's talent for further development. I thought such a course, at a large publicly listed technology company, would be focused on management principles one would expect in an Executive MBA. Particularly, I thought we'd learn the ins-and-outs of hiring and firing people; not that I had any interest in the tactful way of telling someone their career is over. To my surprise, it was a program designed to focus on yourself. A better and deeper understanding of who you are.

Our first assignment was reading *Start with Why* by Simon Sinek[1]. Surely, this book would be the "WHY" on firing people? Again, to my surprise, it was a deeper investigation into finding purpose, covering why a company would have a mission statement and the power of knowing your purpose in daily execution. After the reading assignment, we were broken into groups of four, and over the course of the next few weeks, we'd all uncover, develop, and refine *our* WHY statement.

Every setback is an opportunity to question yourself and become a better person.

Your WHY is nothing more than a reflection upon your past.

A pause in life is essential for you to take inventory and understand the past actions that have occurred in your life. It will give you a foundation to move forward. It opens up the closet for analysis on why things are the way they are in your current state. They may be negative, they may be fearful, sacred, and ugly. Your reflection upon these times will be redeeming. They'll provide you closure and clarity. You can't fully focus on accomplishing anything of substance in life without understanding your past and using that foundation to move mountains going forward. You have to dig deeper than you have ever done before, and you have to get really fucking honest with yourself. If you don't, this whole process will not work.

I didn't fully understand how or why I went to the Academy, nor really how I made it through the rigors of acceptance to graduation. In uncovering my WHY, it gave me a chance to fully dissect every action that led me along the way. It uncovered the power of my subconscious and how I used repetitive prayer and manifestation to see this dream come true. Your WHY will unlock something inside of you. It will open your eyes and shine light onto your ability to manifest the world around you.

Unlocking your purpose is the first ingredient in *The Recipe*. How can you move forward in life without understanding where you came from? If you've never taken the time for reflection before, this is how you uncover your purpose and get your first ingredient.

Steps:

List out two to three moments in life that were incredibly joyous: moments of achievements that stuck with you. That resonated to the point you can feel the reverberations still to this day. Moments that when you look back, these were a time of great pleasure. An accomplishment or sentimental moment that was unforgettable.

- There are of course defining moments in life that 'should' be on this list: birth of a child, wedding, graduation, engagement, etc. I challenge you to also think of something that was sentimental, that touched you, that wasn't worthy of photos and applause. Perhaps a kiss with a lover, a dance, a conversation with a friend or stranger—

that made your hairs rise. Your first A on a test or in a class. Your first award in school as a child or medal/win in sports.
- I choose the word challenge with great care because discovering the happiest defining moments in life can be the hardest to recognize when in the pit of despair.

List out two to three moments of sorrow and failure: past regrets. Times of pain. Moments that crushed you. Left you defeated. Times that you felt truly like shit. Death of a loved one, grand mistakes you've made, moments of soul crushing hurt.

- Oddly enough, coming up with my moments of hurt were actually quite easy. When you fail enough, you have these feelings on speed dial. You can call them at ease with your rolodex of prior defeats, and this is why so many of us remain stuck for years.

Add those moments on a timeline with bullets for each period.

- Put the highlights in life above the timeline.
- Put the lowlights in life below the timeline.

You'll now have a timeline of your life with the most memorable and impactful moments of your recorded history. Your first reflection of the traumatizing and effervescent instances which helped form who you are to this day. You'll see your life, progress from these moments, and see where you fell and where you succeeded. This timeline will speak to you as a narrative of what made you who you are.

With each instance, write and list key parts of each moment:

- Who was with you?

- Where were you?
- How did it make you feel?
- What were the events that led up to this moment?
- How was life different after this?
- What is the importance of this particular event in your life?

Think about this, of all the moments in life you could choose, you came up with these five. Why? What was so defining in this instance that it still resonates for your recollection all this time later?

With each question, you'll notice a theme starting to form. Something about these events will call out to you. For every time you rose to the occasion and every time you faltered, there will be similarities. The attributes of these events will tie into each other. From here, you've now taken the time to document, write, and acknowledge the most defining moments of your life. You've reflected upon yourself to uncover the ebbs and flows of critical junctures in your life's story that have formed who you are.

With each moment detailed, you can understand any similarities between the moments. Key steps you took, either with people, action, time, or place, that led to your successes. And the events which led up to a moment when you've failed.

Really think about this for a moment… We often reflect on times of pain with anger. Have you actually ever looked at to this same moment and dissected the surroundings which led here? Have you ever asked yourself how this moment made you feel and then documented this feeling with pen to paper and posted it out into the world? Human beings carry so much emotional baggage, we damage our body and our mind with toxicity over traumatizing events, yet never asked ourselves how this made us feel or why this was a memorable event in life.

The same goes for our successes. I'm sure we've all fallen victim to "reliving the glory days," but how many poor souls beat themselves up every day for a mistake they've made in the past and never spend a moment to think of their achievements? Children and young adults are particularly prone to this sort of anxiety. They see another person with "something" and through no fault of their own, without enough worldly knowledge, they beat themselves up as failures or "not good at anything."

Imagine if you as a parent actually beat your child up with the words you say to yourself, and then asked your child "How does this make you feel?" Could you even do this to your child? Well, every time you critique yourself over and over again with disempowering words you are hurting and abusing your own inner child.

This is the power of reflection. Take the time out to really think of these events. Write them down. Keep them with you. The uncovering you find about yourself will truly be remarkable. You might be amazed by the story of your life. You'll have diagnosed the areas of pain and will be aware of future mistakes. You'll see and understand where you succeeded before, then make conscious decisions in the future of recreating this same success and achievements. You'll understand the people in your life that were so important, and that they were there for this defining time.

We all have a purpose in life. If you're a living, breathing, conscious human being, you have a purpose. In fact, your purpose has already been defined, you just need to find it. You need to connect the dots of the defining moments in your life and paint a picture of who you are. We all have a past. This past has defined who we are today. It's been influenced by the people, places, and climes that we were subjected to during our upbringing.

Finding your purpose is not coming up with something new.
It's piecing together who you already are.

With the critical moments in your life now mapped out, you can start on your purpose. Your purpose statement is simple and broad. In two parts, it ties in the people and events which shaped your life and your outlook for the future.

MY PURPOSE: *To connect with others and forge new paths in life*

Background: My purpose came through the following defining moments in my life:
Peaks in life:

- Graduation from the Academy -> pinnacle in life
- Life of service in the Marines and deployment abroad -> fulfilling lifelong dreams

Pains in life:

- Death of Father -> loss of the reason I pursued a life of service
- DUI—was confronted by Major Cook (USMC Commanding Officer) -> feeling of letdown, feeling I betrayed my commander

These above events in life brought out the following themes: visualization, manifestation, service, let down, no regrets, and connectedness. They led to the reason why I would do anything: *to connect with others*. Those days of being lost as a child to finding each group of friends in all my life's journey is a key and defining part of my purpose. My reason for a life of service, due to my connection to my father. From the partying to the Academy, to the Marines, to Iraq, to a weekend in the county: *forge new paths in my life*. Every story, good or bad, up or down, that played a defining role in my life is the reason for making my purpose statement.

After you've understood your meaning and purpose and how

every event and occurrence in your past has molded the person you are, then you can begin to define what your WANT is in life. Your why—this is your inventory. You need to take an inventory of your life. Only then can you move forward and progress in life.

Your progress will be your WANT.

---

1. Simon Sinek is a British-American author and motivational speaker. He is the author of five books, including *Start with Why* and *The Infinite Game*.

REFLECTIONS

REFLECTIONS

INGREDIENT II – YOUR WANT

"For a few weeks, I started each morning by writing 'What do I actually want?' at the top of a blank page. It's surprising how useful it is to keep asking the same question. Each time, my answer became more precise. Once I knew what I wanted I turned it into action steps." – James Clear

Mission: this will be your mission statement. This is your task from your superior. It is the foremost paragraph of your order. It is a clear and direct statement of what your unit must accomplish.

After you've understood your meaning and purpose, and how meaningful and impactful major events in your past have come to mold the person you are, then you can begin to define what your WANT is in life.

Your purpose is your inventory. You need to take an inventory of your life. Only then can you move forward and progress in life.

Your progress will be your want

I came across the power of a "WANT" while reading *Think and Grow Rich* by Napoleon Hill.[1] Published early in the 20th century (1937), while our nation was going through the struggles of the Great Depression, it served as a guide for hope. Quite suiting as we've suffered the Great Recession from the fall of the housing market in 2008–2009 and are still navigating the waters post the financial dismay that's wreaked havoc to millions. Our country and the world have been torn to shreds, many losing their homes and only stores of value.

Combined with the COVID-19 outbreak in 2020–2021, eerily familiar to the bubonic plague that swept through our nation in 1900–1904, we are at a time of great peril.

History may not always repeat itself, but it certainly rhymes

Following the plague our world saw the First World War. Following the depression of the 20th century our world ushered in World War II—there were certainly echoes of the repetition and rhymes. Make no mistake, the struggles we endure, whether financial or health, turn people to hate and death. The great masses concoct and formulate that their current demise is brought on by someone other than themselves. Further, a clouded and judgmental mind which is easily prone to manipulation concludes the best option for exiting their perilous state is the conquest of others. To capture what others may want.

This is the power of having a WANT. Without it, you'll be at the mercy of the world WANTS to force upon you.

Now, more than ever, a need for a true and undying WANT can help any who struggle. It provides focus, strength, hope, determination to pull through adversity. It guides you in uncertainty. It serves as your friend and mentor while you are lonely. It acts as a shining light during the darkness.

Nothing is more powerful than wanting something

It provides you access to the untapped and unused resources of your mind and subconscious. It forces the world around you to provide the resources necessary to achieve *your* WANT, and that's what this book is about, *your* want. Finding it, discovering yourself and uncovering *your* want, then helping you get there. The pursuit of what's meant for your destiny.

After discovering this power while reading through Napoleon Hill's classic, I often would think about what my true WANT was. I would spend nights pondering what my life would be like once the WANT is achieved and think if that was the life I wanted to live. I'd go through multiple revisions to think if my WANT suited myself and my family. I'd think of the outcomes it would bring and the impact to the immediate supporters around me: family and friends. How it would impact my conscious self and then determine if this was the person I wanted to be in life. My WANT inevitably would take me some time to finalize, and that is okay! Everyone will come across their true WANT when the time is right. It took me several months; it took Napoleon Hill six months. It may take you a year. In the end, the time it takes to conclude what you truly WANT is meaningless.

The most important part of the WANT, after its determination, is bringing it to life. It first needs to be written down. The only part which will make your WANT formulate into reality is if it can be seen by others. Exactly as the Op Order is written down.

THIS DOES NOT MEAN YOU HAVE TO SHARE IT IMMEDIATELY.

However, if no one can see your WANT, if it lives in only your mind as a thought passing by, it can easily be as forgotten. Taking your WANT and putting it to paper makes it come alive. It is forever etched in history. Scholars can study YOUR WANT and its purpose, its power, for millennia to come. The world is aware that this WANT is for you. The world can now begin to surround you with the resources necessary to aid you in its conquest.

After your want is formulated, written and etched in history and your mind, the only thing left now is repetition. You must think about it daily and say it aloud. Your voice and mind need to convey to the subconscious your commanded intent. Exactly as a Marine leader receives an order, formulates a plan of attack, and conveys this order to the next link down the chain of command—your WANT is your MISSION statement of life.

Your intent for your WANT is exactly the same as the COMMANDER'S INTENT for the order.

This is the most important part of the Recipe: YOUR WANT

Your WANT is your mission statement in life. Exactly as the mission is the most important part of the five-paragraph USMC Op Order, your WANT is the most important ingredient. The mission you give a unit of Marines holds with it the power to command death and destruction. With the power of your mission statement, you hold the power of life in your order. The ability to take life and also the ability to put Marines lives in the face of possible death. This same power holds true for your WANT in life. It has the power of life and death over yourself. It will determine what you achieve and bring to this world with your limited time here. This is why it has to be yours and yours alone. This is why it will take time, weeks, months, possibly years for you to come to decide what this WANT is in your life. For, once it's formulated, your life will now be at its mercy. Your time and those around you will be consumed by the intent of seeing it come to fruition. Make no mistake of its power and the determination it will give you once it is created. You carry with it the power to create and manifest your imagination into the real world.

Everything else in your ORDER, same as everything else in your plan for life, is second in importance to your WANT. This will ultimately determine any future successes or accomplishments you have in life. They either will be in line with your WANT or will be a pitstop on your road to its achievement. This is why you need to spend a great time and energy on its formulation. It has to be your WANT. It can NOT be for anyone else. Not for your parents, your family, nor society. For, everything you do now and when your WANT is achieved will feel as if your time and resources were either wasted or contributed to its accomplishment.

Once you understand that YOUR WANT is truly yours, you'll also stop second guessing whether it's appropriate or not for life. Do not let the world CONvince you that WANTing something is egotistical, selfish, self-righteous, or even greedy.

FUCK whomever seeks to provide judgment on something you have determined you WANT in your life.

It means only two things for those that seek to judge:

1. They have no want, no dream, no goal of their life, no MISSION statement.
2. They failed in the pursuit of their own want, thus will stop others along their way.

In either event, these people cannot contribute to your belief in your want coming alive.

It is truly eye-opening for yourself once you have your WANT. Especially, when you start your pursuit in life. It will feel all your previous judgments, your greed, your confusion and envy you had in life will fall. Where you saw barriers, you will now see opportunity. You will be open and clear minded. You will also see others on their way to their WANT and you will be happy for their success. You'll see they are guided by a belief and INTENT to command the world around them. You'll share your ideas and your WANT with likeminded individuals. Their inspirations and execution may help you. If nothing else, they'll be happy to share their WANT with you and you'll be united in a pursuit of life to make the world around you provide for you and others. This will in turn open your eyes and mind to more powers that can be provided.

I will honestly admit, even harder than determining your WANT is sharing it. We now live in a society where we think everyone must be in line with what society deems proper. We've turned words like etiquette and political correctness into hate speech which is leveraged for us to condemn others rather than condone the free thought of humanity.

We are all individual and free thinkers, anyone who seeks to judge your want is no ally in your pursuit

This is also a second nature power of your WANT; it will expose those around you. The world will become quite clear. Your friends and family will immediately be exposed as your ally when you simply state your WANT and your INTENT on how to achieve it. Then you'll either know they have no WANT of their own or whether the world has sent them to aid you in your pursuit.

I comment to you now, do not worry, their judgments will be as quickly forgotten as the clouded confusion you had in the past. For once you're on your path and you see the glory ahead of you, the naysayers passing by are like leaves blowing in the wind. No roots, no direction, no connection. They'll appear to you as mindless beings, bouncing at the whim of the surrounding world like a leaf in the air. You'll observe them, for a brief stop. But it will be nothing more than a fleeting moment of your life. As you are now on your true path in life, your extolled walk of destiny.

Take a moment, think about someone in life who does not have a dream. Really think about it. What are they doing? They're eating and drinking and breathing the same as you and me, but their mind is filled with what random and curious thoughts. Everything that comes in must be as easily forgotten as it has no purpose. Your conscious mind and your subconscious seek to serve you, how can they aid your ambitions if you have none?

How I came across my WANT

You have to paint a picture of the life you want to live. You need peace, quiet, darkness, and time to paint this picture in your head. When you go to sleep at night and wake in the early morning before sunrise. Close your eyes, close your mind, and ponder in wonderment what the ideal picture-perfect life is for YOU! Not the life your parents wanted, nor the life your significant other wants, but yours. What is YOUR IDEAL life that you want to live? Put this picture of YOU living and breathing this very lifestyle as it's destined to happen. The future manifestation of yourself will come to specific detail in your mind. This will be your WANT in life, your mission.

You WANT needs to be an obsession. It needs to be specific. It needs to be a BIG, HAIRY, AUDACIOUS GOAL (BHAG) in life. Your WANT will come to define you, so make sure it's powerful. It will consume you, as it should. It has to be absolutely yours! It cannot be for anyone else and cannot be for something arbitrary, like, "I WANT world peace, or I WANT to end COVID," or some other bullshit. It cannot be something of value. It has to be measurable. It has to have an end and an outcome in life. It has to be achievable and attainable.

After your WANT is clearly formulated, written, and repeated daily, you'll see the world around you begin to open. I encourage you NOT to think about how you will get your WANT nor how you will achieve your WANT. I only ask you to consistently repeat your WANT, preferably aloud.

The world will provide the rest over time.

Your subconscious will provide.

You command it with your intent.

How you get there may not be as determined as of yet. How could it be? How can the world provide you the means to achieve your WANT if it's barely heard of it from you? You've only recently brought it to life and commanded its arrival into the world and written it onto paper.

You must expect the natural world to take time to provide the path. The path will come in many ways. I cannot begin to explain how the opportunities will start. Each time something good or beneficial or "lucky" an instance may seem; you'll see it as the world is providing. You'll then realize the power you've had by commanding your WANT to the world. Over time and repetition, the stars will begin to align. You'll then grow and realize these events are all in tune to help you. It will be glorious, even more so than any blind luck or lottery that can hit because it will be your manifestation come to life.

You'll explore, test and fail at many things. You will hypothesize, test, and find unlikely outcomes. Each life experiment you take will be another patch of road layered into the concrete of your life en route to your destiny. Each time you try and fail, you'll know that this path is helping you to get to your WANT. Every failure you now endure, you'll be utterly convinced of its purpose to aid you. To close doors in order for you to determine what is your path in life. The adversities you suffered early in life will be seen as the stepping stones they should have been. The pains you've endured, the PITYS you use to take on yourself will be dropped when you're in pursuit of your WANT. You will forget them as blockers as easily as you forgot the harm they used to bring. The NAYSAYERS and the pain endured will go from a chink in your armor to a strength. You'll see yourself and understand that you were battle tested in the field of life, not harmed. Where you were wronged and pained, you'll now realize you were strengthened. Every previous hardship in life was to prepare you for pursuing your WANT.

All In

Your WANT is your mission statement in life. Exactly as the mission is the most important part of the five-paragraph USMC Op Order, your WANT is the most important ingredient. This is the level of determination it takes to succeed in life, that you have to give life. This is the level you need to be committed to pursue your WANT. This is the level it takes to accomplish your WANT in life, it's all in.

It's all consuming, it's pure relentless pursuit.

This is the power of *The Recipe*; it forces you to instill your subconscious with what you want. It forces a habit of positivity. It takes away the ability to fill yourself with self-doubt and loathing. It takes away your fear, if and when you use it.

If you are consistently filing your subconscious with repetitive reinforcements of your WANT and your strengths, there is no room in your daily life for negativity. It takes away your anxieties, your unease, your worry, your loss—and ignites the greatest tool we're armed with as humans in this world—our subconscious.

The subconscious forces the mind and the world around it to bend to your wants. This is immutable. This is fact. If leveraged, recited, and practiced daily—it is impossible not to achieve your goals in this life. Whatever they may be.

Your subconscious does not know any better! The fear you feed it, the worry, the shame, the unknown, it has no navigational guide if these are good or bad thoughts. As humans, we can't help but worry. *The Recipe* is the cure for our natural born proclivity to fear. It will lift your mind and force your body to execute at an unthinkable level. It's scientific. Your body will adhere to your mind. Your mind will adhere to its programming. Its programming will be determined by writing by the subconscious, and that programming language is *The Recipe*.

Balance is a carefully widespread word we use to steal away your dreams. The key point of balance is that you need to manage multiple fronts and efforts.

This is exactly in absolute contradiction to your WANT.

There is nothing great in your life you'll achieve if you live a balanced life. You need to GO ALL IN.

Your WANT is not a balanced position. It is your point in living. We have one life. That's it, one life to live. That makes your WANT singular. You can only achieve this one thing in your life.

What is it?

What do you WANT?

Can it, and will it change? Yes, absolutely.

Clearly, after you achieve it you'll WANT to do something more, further, and redefine yourself as your life changes.

For those of us who don't know we're in a shit position, it looks like this:

1. You don't have a want.
2. You're not chasing your want.
3. You've given up on your want.
4. You don't even know you have a want.

Really take a second to look at these four positions.

First position: If you're living life, and do not WANT anything, then quite possibly what is the point of living life?

To live in balance and harmony?

Is this the lie you're telling yourself?

Is there nothing you want to do, accomplish, achieve, see, feel, live in this world that you do not WANT to do anything?

This is the absolute first step in realizing you're in a shit position.

Not having a WANT or desire.

Second position: If you do have a WANT, are you actually making decisions, daily, that are in line with what you WANT? Ask yourself this. Every day.

Does this decision help me get closer to my WANT?

Now, I'm not saying that we are perfect, and we don't make bad decisions, but on a macro level, take a second to think about the daily decisions you make.

Are they formed out of a bad habit picked up years ago: over eating, over drinking, smoking, over sex, cravings, FOMO,[2] envy?

Are your daily decisions based upon your former self that did not have a WANT in this world?

Now that you've clearly defined your WANT and taken the necessary steps to write it down, pronounce it to the world, and repeat it daily—are your future decisions in line with this WANT?

This is a very critical point to writing down your Recipe and reciting it daily. It forces you to make good decisions based upon what you WANT in life. It takes away the human error for you to skip, cheat, or otherwise not pursue something you WANT in life.

Third position: This is a very difficult point in your life. Nothing can be worse than having a WANT, chasing it, failing, and then NOT having a further WANT any more.

This hurts.

This is the epitome of failure: giving up.

Now, people, circumstances, and the world change. Constantly.

Your WANT may, no... WILL change, but you have to be honest with yourself and your WANT in life. When you change your WANT down the road in life, just know that's okay.

We all WANT different things as time changes.

The mother/father who's only WANT in life was to own a home because this was their level and criteria for success. After they achieve their WANT, do they stop living their life? No, they redefine.

The athlete who's spent his childhood and formative years pursuing a life as a professional who suddenly gets hurt, injured, or otherwise incapable of playing—does he give up his want or redefine?

These are very critical points in your life where you need to make an educated and conscious decision about what it is you WANT in life.

Think about where you're at, what you're chasing, and why it is you have this WANT.

Your INTENTION is the next step in understanding yourself and how you plan to execute on your WANT.

My Want: $25M net worth

1. Oliver Napoleon Hill was an American self-help author made famous during the Great Depression (1930s) for publishing *Think and Grow Rich*, which has been one of the bestselling books in the development genre.
2. FOMO is Fear Of Missing Out, made famous by the Reddit investing community.

REFLECTIONS

REFLECTIONS

INGREDIENT III – YOUR INTENTION

What is intention?
Intention is a mental state that represents a commitment to carrying out an action or actions in the future. Intention involves mental activities such as planning and forethought.

Commander's Intent: this will describe in three components how you specifically want the mission to be accomplished. It will give your intent to your Marines.

As the Commander of your celestial body, you are solely in charge. You are the dictator of your actions. Your thoughts, emotions, and events in your life may feel uncontrollable at times. You cannot control the natural world nor the people who come across you in this journey, but your reactions to the outcomes of what transpires in your life make you overall responsible. With this level of responsibility, you have intent.

What is your desired end state in life?
What is your method of exploitation?
These all detail how you want to achieve your WANT.
Once your WANT is clear, concise, and transcribed to paper, your

INTENT will be the next ingredient in your Recipe. Your INTENT may go through several revisions. Your WANT will never change, until it's fulfilled or otherwise you are incapable of change. You can think of your INTENT as, "What do I want to do in life?" You can further mold your INTENT to ensure it's aligned with your WANT. I WANT something out of life. This is how I INTEND to live my life. This is what I INTEND to do with my life.

Take a second to ask yourself this question: "Have I ever had INTENT before?"

I can tell you, and I confess, as a young Marine, my INTENTIONS were always around how much alcohol I'd like to consume on a weekend. It was terrible. Damaging to both mind and body. This is the downside of intention if it's used for negativity.

Think of the times something bad has occurred in your life. Ask yourself, what was your intention prior to this event? Then, did this event unfold as intended? I can almost assure you, whenever something bad in life has occurred, it was preceded by a negative intention.

I'm not referring to the unfortunate occurrences that we all have to endure such as the car crash, weather storm, company's performance which led to your layoff; no, I refer to the times, if you've ever been in trouble. I'm hoping there are many well-intended souls that have not had to face the trouble, either with law or finances, but, for the rest of us with previous mistakes, all trying to learn from our past aggressions, your intent can be the root cause.

Now that you're aware of the power of your mind and you can control the outcome of your actions. Think about what positive things you want to achieve with your intention.

Quite simply, most of us have never had the chance to really think about what we want to do with life. We've come across the power of intention before, either with people, circumstances, or short-term engagements. I'm sure we've all had intentions with a partner or lifestyle. Perhaps even the type of cars we INTEND to drive.

However, say this to yourself, "I intend to do _____ with my life".

Now, fill in that blank.

Fill it in several times. Your life is long, there will be plenty to do. You can dream up a list of your wildest, most creative dreams and fill in that blank.

This is your soul of painting a picture of the life you want to live.

Think of what this picture looks like.

Think about your daily routine and habits in that life.

You'll wake up, execute your daily rituals: brush teeth, shower, eat, coffee/caffeine, raise kids, then ___.

What do you want to do with this time and space in your picture? Your intention will take you to this place once fully formulated.

Think about all the "What else can I do?" with the power of your intention.

It can surpass just providing a means as a way of living, it can define the person you become in life.

You can have limitless good and positive intentions in life.

Your Recipe will be emboldened by the **INTENTIONS** of your desire.

I INTEND to live a healthy lifestyle.

I INTEND to be a positive contributor to my society.

I INTEND to always be there for my children.

I INTEND to not get upset or lose my cool at colleagues at work (something I've fallen victim to countless times).

I INTEND to be a good husband / father / mother / wife / son / daughter.

I INTEND to travel the world.

I had never intended to write a book and publish my manuscript until meeting my coach and publisher, Dawn Bates at the beginning of 2021. I came across the individual ingredients slowly, one by one, through various uncovering in reading and leadership training.

My WANT came from the findings of Napoleon Hill, in my first and second year at Akamai.

My WHY came through the Next Generation Leadership training (also at Akamai), during my third year.

My intentions came during the COVID lockdown of 2020.

I had my WANT solidified in my mind for some time, approximately twenty months or so.

However, I never had the courage to write it down or share it just yet. It would take me almost two years after uncovering my WANT to write it down. Once this occurred, life changed around me. My course of actions would dramatically look different. Almost as surely as I created my own personal Recipe, with my WHY and WANT, I was already looking for the next adventure.

I would be leaving a very stable, profitable, multi-billion-dollar tech company to go out into the unknown.

During the summer of 2020, our world was being ransacked by a plague not seen in a century. Schools closed, unemployment rampant, people dying. The 1st class privileges we enjoyed prior to 2020 would soon be depleted. Toilet paper would become a scarce asset. Yet, despite this traumatic unfolding, I would make an even bolder move. I would leave a well-tenured and stable technology company (Akamai Technologies) to venture into the startup world and join a Silicon Valley VC-based e-commerce SaaS company.

I will be upfront and deliberate by stating everyone who thinks a technology startup is a guaranteed lotto ticket is delusional, myself included most assuredly myself included.

COVID was such a traumatic time, particularly with an out of work spouse and two children, that leaving a stable future with Akamai seemed like madness. However, **STABILITY IS THE ANTAGONIST OF CHANGE**, and, without change, we can't evolve. Much like choosing to forgo the guaranteed contract to become a Naval Aviator and playing the game of chance as a Marine Officer during a time of dual conflict.

I had to take the plunge into the unknown again, this time with a full family in tow. My wife, forever my partner in chasing my dreams, would be fully onboard with this decision. Why? One may ask would I leave a very lucrative position, during a time of complete economic and social devastation to join a 20-person startup? Because, with my WANT and WHY fully committed, documented, and recited daily, I thought this opportunity was the world speaking to me. This is what I'd asked for. My WANT, financially motivated, would manifest itself in the form of this startup. Clearly, the world was working in my favor. I'd go to this startup, it would go public, and my WANT would be fulfilled.

Easy, right? I mean, how hard is it to take a company public?

After joining the company in September 2020, our CEO (he was the main driver and motivation for me joining, as he'd sold several of his last companies, so I was almost assured we'd repeat his success at this new venture.) resigned less than three months later in November 2020. I cannot begin to explain what regret feels like. Having navigated the financial difficulties exiting the Marine Corps and failing at starting a business, I thought with time and experience in the technology sector I was past making bad decisions.

We are never past making bad decisions!

This time called for more reflection. Heading into the winter and holiday season of late 2020, COVID was peaking at all-time highs, society in full shutdown, this called for READING.

If you've never been moved by a book, by a story, by a novel, you've been reading the wrong books. The right books will change your life. They will change your perspective and understanding. They will fulfill you.

Reading is the pathway to a new life.

After this holiday reflection came clarity. The world has spoken, with no figurehead to navigate your company, I would inflict my INTENTION on life. Work is after all only a means to occupy eight hours of your day. What would I do with the rest of this time? What would I build? What would I write? How would I do this? I dug deep into my past and with the realization that my time in the Marines would serve as a foundation for future creativity, I started on *The Recipe*.

My intention would be to work and write. To publish my thoughts and experiences into the world. This would define my next identity heading into 2021. I would grow the company by day through grit and effort, and by morning and night, I'd write.

During this reflection of 2020, I also came across my next ingredient: HABITS.

My Intention in life:

- Author a bestselling book
- Grow, scale, and sell the company
- Build a world-class brand
- Be a professional investor and trader

REFLECTIONS

REFLECTIONS

INGREDIENT IV – YOUR HABITS

You can't get something for nothing.
The world gives nothing to those who don't give. This is the law of the universe.

Execution: this paragraph will detail how you plan to accomplish your mission.

Your habits are your daily "How to Guide" to go about getting your WANT. They dictate your mind, which will focus your energy. Your habits are going to be based upon your WANT and INTENTION.

They will be the driving force to executing on your mission in life. If your WANT is financially motivated, your habits most certainly will be as well. Same for health or family or healing, your habits will be dictated by your mission.

This law of habits has been reworded a thousand times over the past millennia. It is as old as time itself. Karma, Newton's law (for every action there's an opposite and equal reaction), and the First Law of Thermodynamics: **that you can't get something from nothing**.

Your HABITS are the contribution and action it takes to execute your INTENT and achieve your WANT. The main difference from the physical laws of nature and your powers is this: the natural world cannot transcend, it is limited. It does not have a subconscious divinity. The laws that guide your unconscious are exponential. They return more, immensely, than given.

THIS IS ABSOLUTE!

Your subconscious will force the natural world to provide tenfold over your capabilities. You can't get something for nothing. The world gives nothing to those who don't give. This is the law of the universe. Thirty minutes spent daily on your *Recipe* is given back tenfold. In both speed and intensity, the world will provide faster than you can receive.

Quieten your mind. Silence your thoughts. Quit ruining your own success. Simply give, devote, demand, your only and most important, yet decaying asset is time. Give and you will receive, this is your HABITS.

This is an UNDENIABLE and non-debatable force you have to understand. Every success, miracle, and great achievement recorded in human history was predetermined by an individual who created a concept (WANT) into their mind and defined their purpose to existence and through sheer willpower, putting their intention to work.

Now this is the part that no one is going to tell you about. The pursuit of your WANT is scary. It has to be scary and is going to be scary. It is death defying. Once your PURPOSE and WANT have been defined, and you know your INTENTIONS, every second of the day spent NOT chasing this path will feel like a second wasted. Worst of all, you will know this. You'll be consciously aware that a minute of mindless minutia will be wasted to the hourglass of time.

Your confidence and conviction will be resolute. The judgments and fears you once carried, will now become meaningless. They'll be the forgotten dreams you can't seem to remember when you awake from sleep. They'll be dismissed as quickly as they were conceived. You will walk like a butterfly bouncing from clouds, immune to the laws that hold others back. The powers of anxiety, fear, confusion, lack of focus. These once speed bumps will be wafts of wind passing you by.

Your dreams will scare you, as they should. They'll give you anxiety at night. Your mind, ruminating about the possibilities of the life in front of you, will run like a hot engine thriving to be redlined. The life you can live is right in front of your very grasp.

Your HABITS only require thirty minutes a day! They will focus your mind on what you WANT. These are the tools prescribed as a blueprint to building the life you envision. The prescriptions listed in this book are not made up nor fictional. They are Laws of the Universe. They control your everyday conscious living, as do the Laws of Gravity and Relativity. The universe will provide you with all the facilities to achieve.

THIS IS AN UNDISPUTABLE LAW.

It owes you. If you give, it will provide. Your HABITS are your thoughts, your conscious, your time, your focus, your energy are all that it asks in return.

Your PURPOSE and your WANT are mechanical designs to coerce your thoughts into concrete manifestation of what the UNIVERSE should give you.

Follow this plan. It is by design, infallible. Leverage your strengths and feedback loops to accelerate your pursuit like course corrections on your drive through destiny.

The is the hardest part about the pursuit. The part everyone knows, and everyone hides. They hide it, because as much as the world conspires to help a being in the pursuit of their bounty, to protect you from getting hurt. They pity you; they feel sorry for you, so rather than tell you how hard the path is, they show you their "things." They think their stuff will inspire you.

Feedback Loop

It's very important to understand the importance of repetition and continuous inoculation of your mind. Progression is constant. The pursuit is nonstop. There are roadblocks on the way. Hurdles, detours, timeouts, sink pits, strays, and enemies along this path. Repetition of the loop is vital to keeping you energized and recharged. It gets stronger over time, like a muscle being worked daily. Your subconscious will build and make your dreams a reality the more you enforce your WANTS into its dimension (purview).

YOU MUST IMPOSE YOUR WILL.

This is the job of the conscious; to do, to command your subconscious with your WANTS, and like a robot at your beck and call, it will provide.

The role of the subconscious is to provide and figure out a way to bring the world into your path and reveal you WANT into reality. The subconscious commands all the elements of the cosmos.

This is fact!

This is the great secret. This is the divinity of our soul. Your subconscious has the power to control the universe.

*Note here: It has this power, but, unlike your conscious mind, you can't command it with physical or mental ability, you have to feed it.

The continuous feedback loop is the synergy of your Recipe that activates the power of the subconscious, like the spark required to trigger a nuclear reaction. The feedback loop is the great initiator. Like the **BIG BANG** which created all elements hurtling through space, the divinity of human beings was created with the power to control these elements and harness its power. The divine nature of being human, homo sapiens, we were born with this power. All of us.

Never known, never revealed, never believed—**THIS IS YOUR AWAKENING!**

This is your godsend. The revelation that you can control the universe with your subconscious. This book, *The Recipe*, is the guide that gives you the instructions to control this power.

"HARD WORK, DEDICATION" – Floyd Mayweather

These three words are the mantra of perhaps the greatest boxer of our generation. They define his mindset. They are the key to his success. Three words, repeated constantly, are the benchmark of what made his achievements possible. A Michigan native, with both father and mother addicted to drugs, he'd go on to become an Olympic Bronze medalist (protested), 15-title champion, and retire with a perfect 50-0 record as the highest paid boxer in history. **Three words did this.**

If your intention is your picture of the life you want to live, then your HABITS are how you get there. They are your EXECUTION. This is your third ingredient. The world is often caught up with goal orientation, with having goals and accomplishing your goals, but what we often miss is the path. The journey we take to our WANT is achieved through our HABITS.

Your HABITS are your path to your WANT

Similar to having INTENTION that is in line with your WANT, your HABITS should reinforce this as well. During my time of reflection, after deciding to impose my intention on the world, I found the power of habits from Dr Joseph Murphy and Gary Keller[1]

My HABITS:

- Habit of wealth
- Habit of success

Habit of Wealth: Every day you wake up, repeat to yourself what will make you wealthy.

- [daily] repeat several times for five minutes.[2]
- "Wealth – Success"

Habit of Success:

- [daily] What is one thing I need to accomplish every day to make me successful?
- Workout every morning.
- [annually] What is one thing I need to accomplish this year to make me successful?
- Finish my manuscript.

---

1. ***The One Thing: The Surprisingly Simple Truth Behind Extraordinary Results*** is a self-help book written by authors and real estate entrepreneurs, Gary W. Keller and Jay Papasan.
2. *The Power of Your Subconscious Mind: Unlock the Secrets Within* Dr Joseph Murphy. Published January 1, 1963.

REFLECTIONS

REFLECTIONS

INGREDIENT V – YOUR AFFIRMATIONS

AFFIRM (verb): state as a fact.

Administration and Logistics: will detail elements to aid in the mission. It will provide information on the rations, ammunition, aid stations, and prisoner of war controls.

After coming across my PURPOSE, I found a particular passage in the readings of Eckhart Tolle.[1] In his poem, he detailed the essence of being present. A needed state to ensure one would not suffer from anxiety (fear) of the future and remorse from the past. Being present has always been a difficult for me.

My mind is always racing, always playing out with what the future will look like and hold. In coming across this poem, it resonated in untold ways that brought calmness to my *Recipe*. If your mind is always living in the future, it also means you're not present and when thinking too far into the future, you concoct ridiculous outcomes which never take place nor transpire.

Not being present has caused me a tremendous ordeal of anxiety in life. Such that I understand the poor choice of coping mechanisms I used to combat the anxiety were to turn to abuse. In all forms: drugs, alcohol, food, doesn't matter if you can't stay present, your mind runs. Sometimes it doesn't stop. Even further, sometimes you cannot sleep because of fear of what will happen in the future. In order to stop the running neurons, you numb them. Slow them down. This normally requires an outside narcotic, particularly if you grew up unacquainted with meditation, breathing and healing.

The passage serves me to conquer this anxiety and to continue using my leading STRENGTH (futuristic) without damaging my mind and body. It is a passage I affirm to myself in order to conquer my critical vulnerability.

The passages to "My affirmation" also has a title. It is something I need to start daily in order to ensure my wellbeing. It is something I need my body and soul in order to have a good day: *Everything will be alright*.

This AFFIRMATION is short, basic, and direct. It's done more wonders than any pill in a bottle could hope for. This, combined with the following AFFIRMATION make up your 4TH INGREDIENT.

Daily Affirmation: **EVERYTHING WILL BE ALRIGHT**

- My Infinite Intelligence and the Infinite Power derived from my belief guide me to health and an abundance of money. So, I believe, so I am. I am worth $25,000,000.
- **I am what I imagine myself to be:**
- **Leader, thinker, creator, builder, do'er.**
- **Father, husband, entrepreneur.**
- **Author, investor, positive professional.**
- I have a healthy, successful, prosperous, and happy family.
- There is no such thing as a free lunch. So, I give, so I receive.
- I give full mental and subconscious attention to my goals, my ideals and ideas, and my business enterprises. My deeper mind supports me in all facets and guides me to my health, wealth, and happiness. The application of these

laws of my subconscious mind are impregnating me with
the ideas of health and wealth and happiness.

The above combination of AFFIRMATIONS were derived from the learnings of Dr Joseph Murphy. He was an author, minister, and student of religious teachings. Ordained in both Divine Science and Religious Science, he would go on to publish *The Power of Your Subconscious Mind* in 1963.

It would go on to become a renowned bestseller worldwide. The findings of Dr Murphy in his writings point to the numerous and countless occasions where, with nothing more than thought and spoken word, people can influence an outcome. In his studies and real-world encounters with believers from all religions: western, American, Indian and Hindu sages, he had borne witness to countless miracles. Healings, survival from certain death, unfathomable recovery, and wild fortune successes. He also recorded perfectly healthy and able human beings lose life and limb due to negative thought and worry. The key ingredient to all of these events, both positive and negative comes down to what we say to ourselves, what we AFFIRM to this world.

Dr Murphy would spend his life dedicated to the teachings of the subconscious mind and the power we hold to influence the outcomes of our lives. Mixed with both religion, thought, prayer, and practice, our everyday statements to the world dictate life.

Recall the ability of your subconscious, it has the power to mold the energy around you. It cares not whether you are telling it the past or what is to come in the future. When you AFFIRM, you state as a fact, in voice to the world, only truth. Once your mind and body hear this, they must abide. Your subconscious is forced to provide this to you. It will command the energy of the universe to give this to you.

Your AFFIRMATIONS, from the moment your voice is heard, and a decibel goes from 0 to .00001, becomes a truth in this world. Whether the AFFIRMATION comes now, tomorrow, or some point in the future, it will happen. Your subconscious cannot, unfortunately, measure time. It does however need motivation. You need to speak to it daily. You need to AFFIRM to it every change you have. Your subconscious is lonely. Without your voice, it will go dormant, like an unused muscle withering away.

As your subconscious takes your spoken voice as fact, it also cannot discern between positive and negative truths. If you worry, if you fear, if you feed it with any forms of destruction, it will ensure this comes to fruition. In fact, your subconscious has the power to mold your negative voice into energy faster than positivity, such as health and wealth. This is because the world surrounds us with negativity. It's easy to find. Your mind can summon this energy instantaneously.

Take a second to think to yourself right now, right as you're reading this, you can probably find and pinpoint the exact person with negative energy in your life. They are so easy to find. Without asking, this person, place, or instance of negative energy flowed through your mind without my questioning. I'll do no more in asking, as I'd quickly ask you to purge this thought just as fast as you brought its recollection.

Please take note of the multiple instances of health in my AFFIRMATIONS. I fully understand and am well aware we all seek success and fortune with our time on this earth. My WANT is purely based upon financial gain, but this ingredient carries with it the power to heal. It has the power to heal those around you as well. You can AFFIRM anything you want in this world. Your WANT is specifically for your life's work, but you carry with you the power to heal others. Heal companies, organizations, families, the masses. You can also AFFIRM to give up, let go of regret. "Sadness, bitterness, all forms of fear"—as Mr Tolle puts it, we can AFFIRM to extinguish these sentiments and emotions.

You carry with you, in this ingredient, unknown power. Not just for yourself, but for your family and those around you. Your power is realized through your last ingredient, your STRENGTHS.

[note: Spoken affirmations are only one way of ensuring your body and subconscious receive a given order. If needed, you can record your affirmations and play them back daily. Both voice and video recordings work. You can also draw, create a picture gram or short reel that visually pronounce your affirmations. From memory, writing your affirmations daily is also another method of unlocking this ingredient.]

---

1. Eckhart Tolle is a spiritual teacher, leader, and bestselling author.

REFLECTIONS

REFLECTIONS

REFLECTIONS

INGREDIENT VI – YOUR STRENGTHS

"On the strength of one link in the cable, Dependeth the might of the chain. Who knows when thou mayest be tested? So live that thou bearest the strain!"[1] – Captain Hopwood

Command and Signal: paragraph contains information on the command element and the communication (signal) plans.

The chain of command in an Op Order will detail information about who's next in line should you perish or be rendered incapable of completing the mission. More importantly, it tells you the hierarchy of the unit. The *Signal* gives instructions for communication throughout the unit during the operation. Your mind and body are the commander as you execute on your WANT. You inherently will have good and bad signals for what you're good at. Your STRENGTHS will also have a hierarchy and dictate what gives you power. When you focus on your strengths, the hierarchy will be emboldened.

Your strengths reinforce your success!

Similar to the feedback loop, the more you focus on your stronger attributes in life, the more rewarding they are and the more you will continue to utilize them and then be rewarded further.

I came across my strengths through the Clifton Strengths assessment[2] and test. Authored by Donald O. Clifton and Marcus Buckingham, I came across the last ingredient in November of 2020. Introduced to the test through an old mentor at Akamai Technologies, Marc Brightman[3] (Director of Pre-Sales) walked me through my individual strengths. It was like a great awakening. Everything resonated with me. Life had so much more clarity after taking this assessment and having a mentor teach me about their prowess. Upon adding my strengths to my daily *Recipe* at the end of 2020, the world changed forever that very next month.

The session I had on uncovering my strengths could not have come at a better time. Just the month prior, our CEO of the company had tendered his resignation. Our small tech startup in disarray, going into the holidays I thought our company would be most done for. Particularly, with COVID at the peak of its rage in winter of 2020, heading into the holidays was a bleak time.

Marc provided me the opportunity to uncover my strengths during this time and weather the storm we had at our forefront. Within thirty days, quite literally before Christmas, a new CEO stepped in, and I would come to find the most powerful investment of our time since the internet. Adding the final ingredient to my Recipe marked its completion. My world turned around in thirty days once I put the ingredients together and practiced, daily, their powers.

Your STRENGTHS are the last piece to self-awareness.

Your personal inventory develops your purpose, your manifestations define your WANT, and it is your STRENGTHS that empower you. Without your strengths, you're partially broken. You are half-defined. You may know yourself, but do you know what makes you strong? What drives you? Your strengths are a part of your genetic code which empower and drive your mind body. I'm not talking about some arbitrary subject in school, I'm speaking to what consumes your mind and drives your personality. Who are you as a person? How do you think? How do you prefer to think? How do you take feedback? How do you give feedback?

Strengths: conscious self-awareness of your strengths are beneficial for two reasons:

1. So you will NOT focus on your weaknesses.
2. To re-energize.

Energizing is a **very big** concept to understand about strengths.

We all live in a connected world, filled with the highest tempo and dramatic egos.

Particularly in the current environment of e-commerce and even specifically mobile commerce, ego is our anti-Christ. It's the destroyer of our self. It ruins our image, confuses our PURPOSE and WANT, then destroys our pursuit to success.

Why?

It's a projection of what you think to a world you don't know. It's against the purpose of self-awareness. The journey of transformation is to become aware, then go onto your pursuit. Ego clouds both sides. It stops your awareness, limits your ability to uncover, then takes you off your journey of the pursuit.

Since our strengths build us and provide energy, there is the ability for energy to be taken away, stolen, captured by others who seek to know no other way of building their false strengths other than taking energy from their surroundings. Most of the time, completely unconscious of their theft, but visible to the everyday looker who's seen this energy-vampire ruin people, organizations, and countries.

You've seen them too before, just never with the context to realize what was actually taking place. They're all around us, in all facets and guises. They are the CYNIC. They are the definition of the EGO. They give anxiety. Think about this in all times and places where you've been almost afraid to see, think, or even come close to someone. They make your blood boil. They bring down your mood.

They rain on a sunny day, and they're completely unconscious of their actions, even in the voice of improvement, betterment and empowerment, they can't see what they do to others. The worst of all, they cannot take feedback.

Think about how much time we spent earlier on how crucial self-awareness is to your pursuit and the absolute necessity of feedback loops for continuous improvement. Feedback, coaching, continuous development of the self all point to allowing others to help us on our path. We open ourselves up to the world and let mentors energize us. They gladly do it because it energizes them to help as well. It's a continuous cycle of giving and receiving that energizes connections and produce exponential energy for the world. This is why it is a feedback LOOP. Energy is given, taken, received, then acted upon, and the path/pursuit is enhanced. It is so enhanced that the energy that emits from the loop is a glowing light on those that come near it.

You've seen that as well, I'm hoping, that positive kismet when family, friends, colleagues, workers, mentors work in conjunction with the feedback loop produces a mind meld. It enhances entire teams; it builds governments and nations. The ability to take in feedback, unbiased of the ego is a monumental step towards self-empowerment, and here, all alone, is the egomaniac, stealing it. Snaking its way into the loop with the utter and unconscious destruction, draining activity. Your strengths will guide you to your WANT. It will be impossible to achieve anything of significant value in life without relying upon your strengths.

For re-energizing, building up your body and soul, you also have to be aware of what depletes energy: cynics and soul-sucking and energy-draining tasks.

My strengths:

- Futuristic – share your visions of a better future.
- Maximizer – strive for excellence and encourage others to do the same.

- Ideation – refine your creativity to inspire and energize yourself and others.
- Positivity – help others see the humor and positive side of life.
- Command – be ready to take charge when others waver.
- Intellection – think deeply; think often.
- Input – keep exploring; always be curious.
- Strategic – always have at least three options in mind so you can adapt if circumstances change.
- Significance – look for opportunities to do important work where you can help others raise the bar.
- Focus – set specific goals with timelines to motivate yourself.

Being conscious and aware of your strengths also serves another purpose, to fulfill and re-energize your body based upon your specific persona.

The opposite of your strengths are your weaknesses. Your weaknesses steal your energy, they drain you. They leave you feeling empty and unfulfilled. Our society has been convinced of providing us feedback in a manner where we think that doing something below average is a **WEAKNESS**. For whatever reason, we think there's some magical line of what society is, we'll call this average, and if you're under this mythical line, you're weak. If you're above it, you're strong. So therefore, I need to tell you your weaknesses and what to fix. Fuck that! No one is here to save you; you have to save yourself by identifying and telling yourself what your strengths and weaknesses are.

You need constant recognition of what you're strong in. No one is perfect in anything, ever. Being aware of your weaknesses is okay. Trying to improve them doesn't make you any better in your strengths. You need awareness of what it is that does NOT bring you energy so you can focus your mind and efforts on what you're strong at.

My Weaknesses:

- Execution, Discipline, Deliberative, Consistency, Comparisonitis.

How to overcome my weaknesses: do something little every day. Work on your WANT at least 15 minutes a day.

- Write down your ideas
- Record (voice memo) your thoughts
- Work out each day
- Put your thoughts into action
- Work on *The Recipe* each day
- Grow the company, each day

---

1. Hopwood, C.B., Royal Navy, published by W.R. Deighton & Sons, London, England, during the World War I era. It is illustrated by etchings by Lieutenant Rowland Langmaid, R.N., depicting scenes of the contemporary British Navy. The poem originally appeared in the Army and Navy Gazette, July 23, 1896.
   https://digital.lib.uh.edu/contentdm/file/get/p15195coll22/1159/1160.pdf
2. *Now, Discover Your Strengths* teaches you how to succeed using your most powerful natural talents. The book gives you practical tools, insights, and examples so you can: understand why strengths are so important to success. Learn how to build strengths using your natural talents.
3. Marc is the head of Media Pre Sales at Akamai Technologies with 19 years of experience. Experienced technical pre-sales and post-sales leader/coach with a demonstrated history of working in the media industry. Skilled in leadership, strengths coaching, content delivery networks, customer experience, professional services, and streaming media.

REFLECTIONS

REFLECTIONS

CLOSING

"There's only one rule to be successful in life. Don't lie to yourself." – Paulo Coelho

Most of us will work. This is the inevitably of the world. A vast majority of us will relish in the day when our waking hours are spent not working. In other words, doing something we do NOT WANT to do, but how many of us are actually reinforcing our mind to provide this life for ourselves NOW?

Back to the story at the beginning of the fleet of souls with no hopes, dreams, goals—WANTS—those in *The Struggle*. How many of us are thinking daily of what we do NOT WANT? Those countless hours in the morning drive, stress of the labors, anxiety over the taxes. Think of how much time is spent impregnating your mind with NON-WANTS. Imagine, with thirty minutes, what the subconscious would think if it were being worked every morning on your WANT. It would be a never seen before refreshment. It would empower your soul with uncontrolled positivity and hope. You slave away your entire life, which has been spent thinking of what you do not want. *"I don't want to work"* … *"I don't want to wake up early"* …. *"I don't want …"*.

The power of your subconscious is so mighty, it's been reinforced with so much negativity it doesn't know what else to provide you. Insert cheesy line here: *If you do what you love, you'll never work a day in your life.* No, unfortunately, you will still work. You still will be anxious for that miraculous day in time when you actually stopped caring. Probably closer to the end of your timeline when the realization comes that you have less days breathing in front than behind. Your cares really start to wane when you hit this realization. In fact, some of us gave up caring that we never actually tried at all!

We were never given the chance to have a realization of the power of our subconscious, no one showed us how to use it.

Like a sponge filled with toxic energy, waiting for relief, waiting to be flexed, this is the empowerment you've been waiting for. Combined with your strengths, your purpose, a specific and detailed WANT, and daily repetition, your subconscious will expand exponentially to provide you the world of your dreams. So much of our time is spent thinking we want things, rather than thinking of the things we want. It is never focused.

Imagine a morning commute to work, we drive by the Porsche, in streaking red, we see it in awe, gasp as it passes us by, and pray for the day that we will one day be afford such a beauty. What we're actually thinking is not of the money or maintenance or depreciation or practicality. All of these conscious thoughts that rule "'good decision" making like having the monthly budget to afford such a machine. We may not be thinking of the money at all. Rather, we're hopeful for the moment in life where we stop caring so much about making sound decisions. We're subconsciously hoping and praying for that day to come where we actually have given up and are "okay" to be making unsound decisions.

We're hoping to actually give up on our financial dreams, such that we'd be okay to spend such currency on a vehicle. Think about that for a moment. How many of us are financially focused now, working, saving, investing, thinking of the miraculous day in the future where we actually stop caring enough about money that we can finally spend it.

You may think you're focused on your inevitable utopian future where your money cushion is enough that you stop caring about it. NO, you're actually just looking to the day that you're so expended of energy and life, that you actually give up caring. This is a sad day for us all.

We're all looking forward to not caring.

Remember, channel thirty minutes every morning and focus on your strengths, your true WANTS, and that millisecond dream will be a smirk on your face as you walk undeterred in your pursuit of your *Recipe*.

With no plan in place, we will break our life for a spur of the moment idea. The millisecond WANT I call it. Now imagine if your WANT was actually powerful enough that you wrote it down? You not only turned that millisecond into a living breathing word. You put it on paper. You added it to your calendar. You spoke it out loud. You verbalized it. You channeled your subconscious to know that this is what your conscious mind wanted. You focused your strengths, daily, for thirty minutes to energize your mind and subconscious, the world would be forced to provide you with that WANT. It would be a guaranteed inevitability.

Are you spending your time chasing these millisecond dreams? These flutters of the moment lapses? Remember, I am not here to judge you, I'm merely to guide you as I was once a dumb ass, as you have read. By controlling the subconscious, leveraging your *Recipe* and turning it into action, these flutters will be smirks on your face when you have self-realization that you can and will do so much more!

You have to understand this: When focused, channeled, built, strengthened, repeated—THE UNIVERSE IS FORCED TO PROVIDE FOR YOU.

This is the great power of our subconscious. This is what every successful person knows. That it is a **guarantee** in life when you focus your subconscious, your innate strengths, granted to us by the spirit of the cosmos, combined with your WHY will act as a supercharger to your subconscious. Repeated thirty minutes daily, it will awaken a giant of epic proportions into

I am an absolute fan of goal setting, scheduled planning, objective setting, but think about this as you go forward. You have a series of goals, probably time based: daily, weekly, quarterly, annually. Then you provide a series of actions to help make these goals a reality. Tasks are added, to ensure incremental achievements are completed to finish these goals. Then, by the end of the timelines, you look back and are hopefully successful. Even the most successful business enterprises and "wealthy" individuals have trouble with such an approach. If goal setting and tasks were enough to help us become successful, the world will be greeted by millionaires on every corner.

The issues with such an approach? You never leveraged your subconscious to help you. Your conscious mind controls your immediate physical nature around you. This is what you see. So, you gave it tasks to *"do,"* tasks to complete. You never spoke to yourself and leveraged the full power at your will. Your subconscious controls all the unseen elements that power our universe. It's at your will, working 24/7, and here, in our very own lives we never tapped into such a miraculous power. Even the best masters of goal setting and task accomplishment are limited on their ability to achieve. They can merely hunt and accomplish fictional achievements.

- Fictional achievements: These things we all thought we wanted, but then realized this is what we thought society wanted of us in order to make us feel special, important, and least of all successful.
- This isn't meant to deter anyone from their goals or accomplishments. This is meant to awaken you to the true underlying power you have at your hands. A focused purpose and want, leveraged with your STRENGTHS and turned into daily spoken repetition, are a cosmic force of limitless power.

- Goal setting is just doing something in your day.

This is the great breakthrough of the 21st century. This is the secret, the magic, the explosion of the limitless power—this is the power of the subconscious. Even for those of us aware of its power, we were never taught how to use it.

This book is the guide.

It's THE Recipe.

The instructions, the field manual, the blueprint to harnessing this power and true achievement of SUCCESS. Some of us can't even define success.

The Chase

My chase started that transformative day in 7th grade when I picked up the book about the US Naval Academy. That defining moment in life gave way to what would be my future. My chase has certainly taken detours along the way. It was definitely not perfect and anywhere far from pretty. When I faltered, the universe somehow found me and put me back on track again. Whether through failure or through family, I've had the privilege to define my chase, to see it clearly, understand it and work in a natural progression towards its completion.

We're all in movement, in motion, progressing, revolving around the earth, the sun, with the moon pulling gravity at us. This means our natural state is meant to be going forward. Our bodies and cells and state of being were designed for this purpose. We all need to be chasing something. If you're stagnant, if you're content, you're in an unnatural state. You're violating the environment and natural law.

Your chase doesn't have to be for wealth, fame, successes, or "more." It can be for health, enlightenment, meaning, restoration, healing, giving. Siddhartha Gautama (Buddha) was chasing enlightenment. Through prayer, stillness, reflection, sacrifice, meditation, he was chasing nirvana. Dr Joseph Murphy, in his consistent and undying work, was chasing the power of the subconscious mind and seeking to distribute its wealth and wonders to the masses. He came across countless stories, miracles of health and recovery.

Your chase is yours, whatever it is! But, you have to have something to chase, you have to be in a constant motion chasing something, and all you have to do is write it down, that's it. You're worthless if you aren't.

The Recipe is a guidebook on your chase.

Your Purpose will remind you WHY you're doing this to begin with.

Your WANT and mission in life will be your destination and your north star, guiding you.

Your INTENTION will be your checkpoints along the way.

Your HABITS will be the daily races and relays you need to overcome.

Your AFFIRMATION will be your recovery, healing, and pitstops.

And your STRENGTH will see you through to the end.

After each chase in life, go find another one, and refine your *Recipe* each time.

I've failed at everything in life, I really have. Failure is the price you pay to determine if you're worthy of the outcome.

Failure is the toll for the ferry crossing the plane of success.

Business, investing, relationships, family, school, leadership, I've failed in every area of my life. The chase keeps me going, knowing that I have to be in pursuit, in motion, in natural progression is the perseverance needed to wipe off the stains of failure.

- The girl who dumped you – she's not worthy of your time.
- The job who fired you – you'll land somewhere better.
- The interview that said no – this is not your path in life. You are not meant to be here.
- Losing people in life – it's a natural progression for those who were meant to join you.

- Losing a business – this was not your calling.

Don't be overwhelmed and let your conscious mind con you into thinking everything in life is a "yes" or that you're meant for everything. You are destined for exactly what it is you're meant for. The chase will be that destiny. Everything has a rhyme and reason for being in its state in your life. Once you're on your chase, this will all make sense, everything will resonate. If you're not in the chases, then nothing will have meaning.

The push for more.

If there is one thing I can share and attest to, it is this: you will never get anything or get anywhere unless you push for more.

My first sales director (Amphenol, 2013) at our global kick off conference took the stage, amongst more than one thousand motivated professionals and left me with this everlasting quote: "Go in there and fight for your unfair share." – Rich Riccitelli. He would go on to become Group General Manager in charge of a $1,000,000,000 plus profit and loss, overseeing six companies and twenty manufacturing locations; congrats Rich! That's what success is and looks like. It's unfair, to those not trying. It's the daily wake up and want for more. It's the *not enough* mindset and attitude. It's the *unfair* amount you desire but don't deserve. No one deserves anything in this world. No one is owed anything.

America only promises us and ensures that we have an opportunity to wake up and try harder. That's it. Our great country just says we'll give you the right to play and compete in the arena, the field of arms, and, if you didn't know it already, and you're living in this country, you're already competing. You're already in the field of battle. If it isn't abundantly clear, every minute of your existence, someone is taking something from you, whether it be through tax, inflation, lower wages, rising living costs, etc. The world is taking from you every minute you breathe. In order for you to push through this already existent headwind, you have to want more.

Nothing will determine your ability to succeed then the sheer perseverance of wanting more. The only way to get more is to continue to push yourself. You remind yourself, your body, your abilities, daily, that whatever you have is not enough. You have to continually find yourself in adversity, in adverse places, in adverse climes and times, in uncontrolled environments where the outcome is not certain, where your future is anything but hazy. If your future is always the "fog of war," you'll continue to always fight through it, or, you'll accept your current place and current standing. The acceptance of your standing determines where you land in life. The day you've mentally and physically acquitted that you have enough is the day you know where you end up in life. It determines your rung on the ladder.

Your race, background, previous accomplishments fail in comparison to the mental mindset and ability to want more. More of everything. Your life, your future, your children's future, your family, your work, your pay, your house, even your type of dog food. Push for more.

Push yourself, daily. Find yourself in adversity. Seek out the places where failure is almost guaranteed and throw yourself in. Embrace being in a shit situation. When all odds are against you, when there is no avenue but up, that's the place you need for success. Life is a series of people shitting on you and when you accept the smell, that determines where your place in life is.

Things like *work, life, balance*—only in this country could we ever think to propose notions that life and balance are inherent and deserved. Go to war-torn Iraq and tell a kid, who's gone through the US invasion, twice, that he needs more "balance." Are you fucking kidding me? He's seen his country demolished, then taken over and raped by ISIS, then decimated through economic poverty. Go explain to him he needs things like a vacation and balance. If you've ever found yourself in a favela, slum, or third world ghetto and tried to explain to its inhabitants' things like "work, life, balance" their confusion and your safety would be put to the test.

REFLECTIONS

REFLECTIONS

REFLECTIONS

EPILOGUE – HOW IT'S GOING

The ingredients to *The Recipe* have been tried and tested. They are leveraged by industry titans and everyday individuals who are making an impact with their time on this earth. I came across the power of these ingredients, and after combining them, with practice and sheer belief in their glory, I transformed my life in one year.

YES! ONE YEAR!

It was difficult to share my WANT. It got me nervous, anxious, and I was frightened to have the audacity of wanting such wealth. In fall of 2020, during the midst of COVID, I told my best friend at a dinner on a Tuesday evening, overlooking Manhattan Beach. This was the first time I spoke of its existence aloud. After this empowering evening, my WANT was made to the universe. It was beyond my mind and now the world heard what it is exactly that I WANTed.

This is all it takes to get the ball rolling.

Following that dinner, I came across the HABIT ingredient. It was the final piece to *The Recipe*. It was the last touch to perfection. Once the HABIT was added, my life changed.

You see, up until that point, my financial decisions had been horrible. I'd left the military, after 13 years, with not a dime to my name. Following the failing of starting my first business, Rita's Italian Ice, it was clear I had no prospect running a company. The failing of Rita's eventually led to my bankruptcy in 2014. Surely, one would recognize their ways and practice fiscal responsibility and discipline. However, I would go on to lose more. In 2016, after transitioning to a new job in the media industry, I would go on to blow up my trading account and lose all my savings. At that time, around $50K. Going into late 2017, early 2018, I once again did not have a dime to my name.

Continuing to work in the tech industry, this instance with Akamai Technologies from 2017–2020, I once again built up some savings and was then hit with COVID. With the sharp drop in stocks in March 2020, I was certain this was the opportunity of a lifetime to load up on undervalued equities and rebuild my portfolio. However, as the stock market went on a ridiculous roar through mid-late 2020, I was actually losing money. I was chasing and going "all in" on very speculative assets, which were too volatile. I ended up losing $70K throughout 2020.

This led me to take a pause in my investments entirely from October to December 2020. During this time, I dug and then dug deeper for purpose. I needed something. Every situation involving finances for my entire life ended up with me losing. How could I walk this earth for 38 years and still be a loser?

This is when I went "all in" on *The Recipe*. I practiced and recited daily. Further, I believed in its power. I believed that the words spoken aloud had meaning to mold this universe. I have witnessed the power of my subconscious in going through the Academy. All I had to do was get back to the basics. Get back to believing, get back to having purpose, chasing a WANT and leveraging the power of HABIT and my own STRENGTHS to execute on my dream.

In mid-December, I was introduced to **Bitcoin**. Having heard of the previous cycle in 2017 which some would say was the biggest recorded bubble in history, led me to believe that it was nothing more than a fictitious currency, but this time was different. The introduction now came by way of my most successful friend, Juan Gutierrez.

Juan, out of the five of us in our "animal group" was by far the most successful. As a college recruited athlete for soccer at University of California Riverside (UCR), following graduation, he went on to commercial real estate in Southern California. Driving the warehouse boom from 2006–2021, he rose through the ranks to Vice President at the age of 36 and had a sizable portfolio to show for his 15 years of success. Hearing his conviction on this particular asset was important to my uncovering.

After the introduction, I started my own research by way of podcasts, YouTube, Twitter, and every social media platform available to understand what was going on with this asset.

From December 2020, Q1/Q2 of 2021, Bitcoin would go on to triple in value, from roughly $20K to $60K by March. A tremendous feat for any asset to triple in three months, one fiscal quarter. As of writing this passage I have every ounce of conviction that this asset is going to $300K by end of 2021. Once this occurs, it would have taken my investment from December of 2020 to a roughly 10–20X. This is the power of *The Recipe*. This is the power of these ingredients. When you are at your lowest, **when you've failed your entire fucking life, *The Recipe* will save you.**

Regardless of the initial investment I started with or the amount I'll end up with, I laid witness to a 10X event in my life. I've watched it unfold, and I was a part of it. To 10X anything in your life is a miracle. It is also the most addicting dopamine rush you can experience. It changes you. It is life changing in itself. All those years, my search for meaning as a child, my search for adventure in the military, would culminate to this success. Those failures, retries, losses, we're all meant for this event. There's nothing like it, to 10X anything in your life, your health, wealth, love, harmony, enlightenment, it's an unshackling event; and once you've found it, it will rewire who you are, and the world will inevitably be a different place as you navigate its course.

Watching this miracle unfold for me led me to share *The Recipe* with you and everyone. If I can go from complete financial ruin, multiple times in my life, and come out and escape COVID with a 10X event, how could I not share this story with you?

Every failure in my life I probably should have stopped. I should have remained conservative. Four decades of failing, how long does it take to realize you're a wreck? The problem was not with my strategy, it was with my mindset and my belief. That's all it takes is belief. It took me forty years to realize this and now I share it with you.

I was not armed with *The Recipe* in all of my past failures. I did not have the energy of the universe aligned to my purpose. I had no **WHY**, no **WANT**, no **POWER**, no **HABIT** and no **AFFIRMATION** to execute accordingly.

How can you do anything in life if you're not in accordance with what you voice to the world and to the universe? Of course, you'd be destined for hardship and failure.

This is why I write, this is why I share: to help you. It doesn't matter how often you've failed in the past or how successful you are now, if you're not armed with these ingredients, you'll be victim to the universe's decisions on your behalf.

When I came across the last and final ingredient, STRENGTH, I thought my Recipe was complete. I added the last portion, and once it was implemented, life suddenly took off. I came across different people and groups and my professional network expanded tremendously. I came across reading and writing differently and my learning process was now different after adopting a growth mindset. I came across an investment that would change my life forever. I found a community that thought different about the way the world's financial system would look in the future. Everything was trending in the right direction. For once in my life, I had the clarity of direction again and could see its fruition play out in my mind. I had a picture of the life I wanted, and it was being painted slowly. All that was needed was time.

The ingredients may have been finished, but *The Recipe* wasn't truly complete. *The Recipe* started working slowly with each ingredient, and faster once I put it together and made it part of my daily routine. I utilized it daily for motivation, therapy, alignment, and healing, but it wasn't complete. During the course of writing a manuscript, much like field navigation in the Marines, you have a fixed endpoint you need to reach, but getting there is the uncovering. While working with my coach and publisher, Dawn Bates, we went through a deep cleanse to find out who I really was and what this story would be about. It was in that time; she gave me the freedom I needed to put this story together. She gave me the freedom to forgive.

Forgive yourself from your past!

The freedom to let go and quit worrying about being judged for what you did, what you'll do and what the world has to hold over you. The power to break the shackles of your past is the final piece to a mindset of success.

Give it up, let them go, release the bad people and energy and experiences of your past. Then your *Recipe* will be ready. More importantly, you'll be ready. Ready to receive the blessings and abundance this universe has to give.

THE DOWNFALL OF VETERANS

This is a downfall of many veterans as we transition to the civilian and corporate world. We forget we have to keep giving. We're always in service. Our watch has not ended. In fact, life after military service means our watch has only just begun. We should all be thankful for what we learned with our previous experiences. They help set us apart in this new world without Military Justice. Thinking our hardships are in our past is nothing but ego.

We all face hardship tomorrow, every human on this planet. The key is to find the right ingredients to make those hardships align to your purpose in life. If you're going to do anything difficult in life, it may as well be in service to your WANT and INTENTION. Your focus should be on your HABIT, led each day by what you AFFIRM to this world. Your STRENGTH is your true nature in life. With its uncovering you find yourself and can align your energy to yourself.

The world owes you nothing. Rather, you are indebted to it. Every breath you take, you receive the energy of life the universe provides, as such you must pay it back. Everything you've done in your life and in your past leading to your present moment is history incurs that debt. The universe wants its energy back tomorrow and the day after.

Any previous accomplishments you may have had in life mean nothing to what you owe tomorrow.

The college you went to doesn't mean anything if you run your business into the ground. The awards you received in the military are of little effect when facing bankruptcy court for bad investments. The discipline you once had to weather through years of training, separation, and combat deployments are nothing if you continue to abuse drugs and alcohol.

Let *The Recipe* be your guide in this next endeavor in life.

Let it aid you. You are not alone in this; you're equipped with the means and faculties to succeed in anything.

Don't pity yourself, hide who you are or run from your past. Instead, dig deep.

Find yourself again, that Marine within you.

With each ingredient, you'll be born anew and have a divine sense of spirit to conquer.

I wish you well in your next life after this awakening.

In service always,
Jake

MY RECIPE
EVERYTHING WILL BE ALRIGHT

My Purpose:

To connect with others, so we can forge new paths and make a positive impact on life.

My Want:

- $25M net worth

My Intentions:

- Author a bestselling book
- Grow, scale, and sell the company
- Build a world-class brand
- I am professional investor and trader

My Habits:

Habit of Wealth:

- Every day you wake up, repeat to yourself what will make you wealthy.
- [daily] repeat several times for 5min.
- "Wealth – Success"

Habit of Success:

- [daily] What is one thing I need to accomplish every day to make me successful?
- Workout every morning.
- [annually] What is one thing I need to accomplish this year to make me successful?
- Finish my manuscript.

My Affirmation:

- My Infinite Intelligence and the Infinite Power derived from my belief guide me to health and an abundance of money. So, I believe, so I am. I am worth $25,000,000.
- **I am what I imagine myself to be:**
- **Leader, thinker, creator, builder, doer.**
- **Father, husband, entrepreneur.**
- **Author, investor, positive professional.**
- I have a healthy, successful, prosperous, and happy family.
- There is no such thing as a free lunch. So, I give, so I receive.
- I give full mental and subconscious attention to my goals, my ideals and ideas, and my business enterprises. My

deeper mind supports me in all facets and guides me to my health, wealth, and happiness. The application of these laws of my subconscious mind are impregnating me with the ideas of health and wealth and happiness.

YOUR RECIPE

MY SELF EVALUATION

My strengths:

- Futuristic
- Maximizer
- Ideation
- Positivity
- Command
- Intellection
- Input
- Strategic
- Significance
- Focus

My weaknesses:

- Execution, Discipline, Deliberative, Consistency, Comparisonitis

How I will overcome my weaknesses: do something little every day.

Work on my "Life's Work" at least 15 minutes a day.

- Write down my ideas
- Record (voice memo) my thoughts
- Work out each day
- Put my thoughts into action -> *The Recipe*
- Work on *The Recipe* each day
- Grow the company, each day

YOUR SELF EVALUATION

WHAT IS HUSTLE?

Hustle is doing something that everyone is absolutely certain can't be done
Hustle is getting the order because you got there first, or stayed with it after everyone else gave up
Hustle is shoe leather and elbow grease and sweat and missing lunch
Hustle is getting prospects to say "yes" after they've said "no" twenty times
Hustle is doing more unto a customer than the other guys are doing unto him
Hustle is believing in yourself and the business you're in
Hustle is the sheer joy of winning
Hustle is being the sorest loser in town
Hustle is hating to take a vacation because you might miss a piece of the action
Hustle is heaven if you hustle
Hustle is hell if you don't

ABOUT THE AUTHOR

Jake Cosme attended the United States Naval Academy (class of 2005) and went on to serve as a Marine Corps officer from 2005 - 2012. Rising to the rank of Captain, he would deploy twice with 3rd Battalion / 7th Marines (3/7) to Ramadi and Al'Qaim, Iraq in support of Operation Iraqi Freedom.

He is a graduate of The Basic School (TBS), Infantry Officer's Course (IOC), Scout Sniper Unit Leaders Course (SSULC) and Ground Intelligence Officers Course (GIOC).

This is his first book and he leads pre-sales teams in the Tech and Finance world. He is a familiar fan of a cold IPA, and will not stop chasing the dream.

If you have purchased a copy of this book, we would love for you to send us a selfie of you and the book on your preferred platform:

facebook.com/RealDawnBates
instagram.com/realdawnbates
twitter.com/realdawnbates
linkedin.com/in/dawnbates

...so we can thank you in person.

With love and gratitude,
From all at Dawn Publishing

www.ingramcontent.com/pod-product-compliance
Lightning Source LLC
Chambersburg PA
CBHW021436080526
44588CB00009B/555